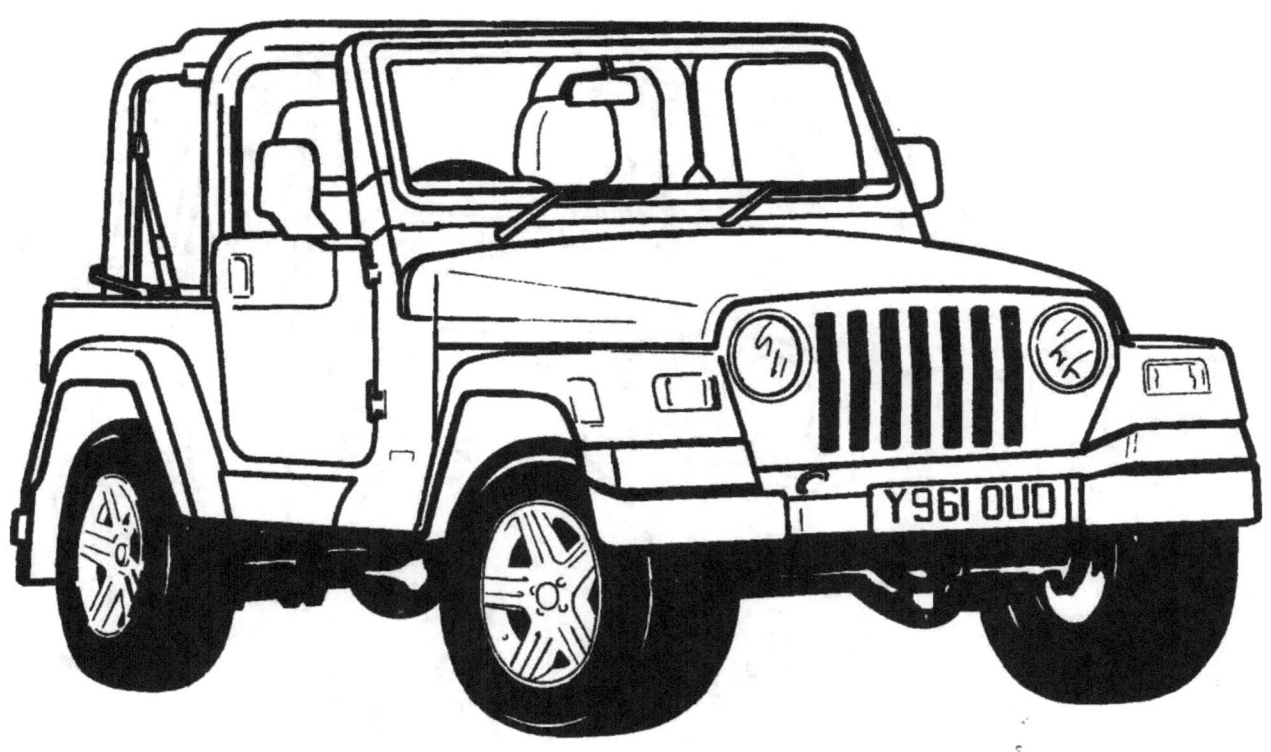

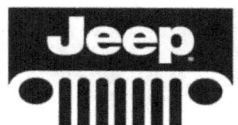

JeeP - Wrangler
1986 - Present Day
Made in USA

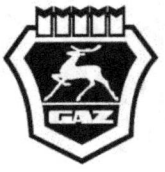

GAZ - Tigr
2005 - Present Day
Made in Russia

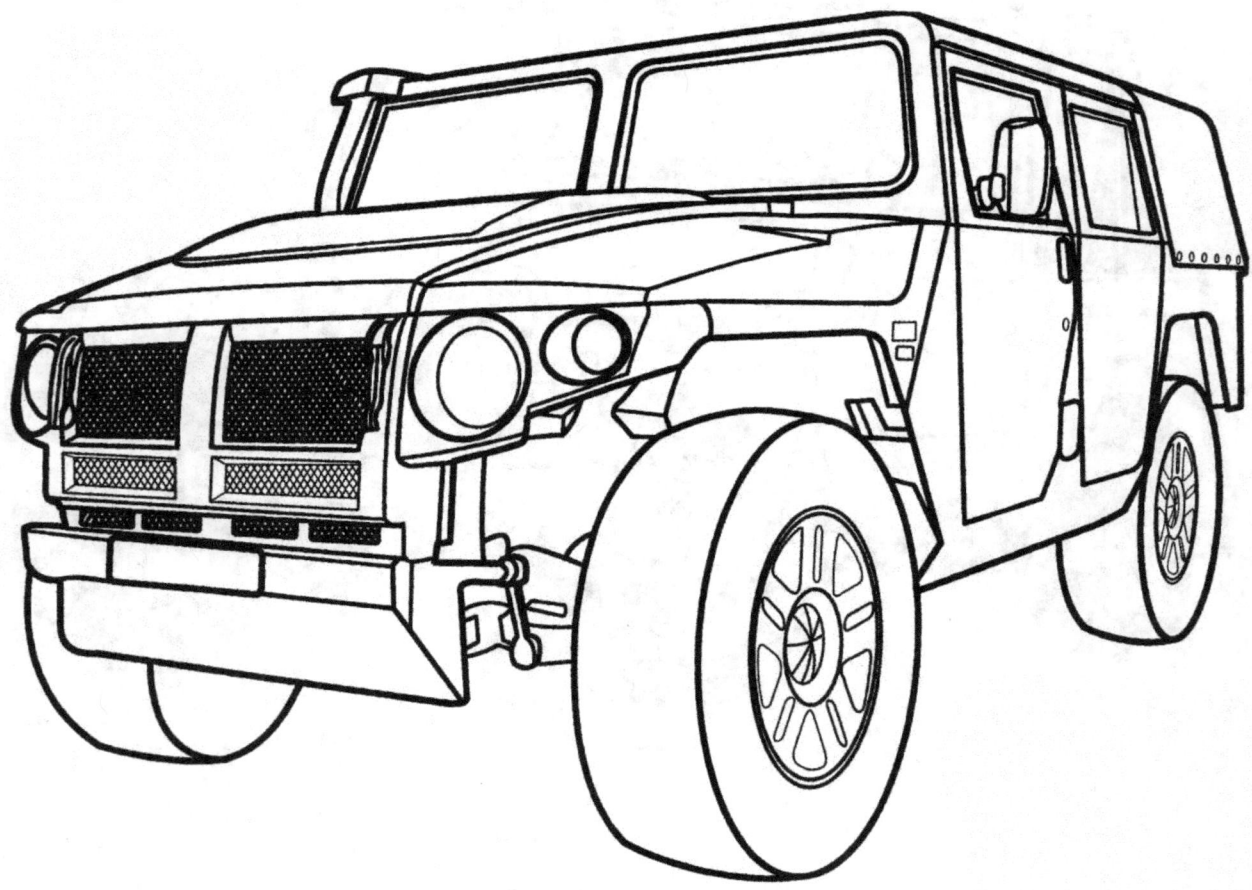

MITSUBISH - 3000GT
1990-1995
Made in Japan

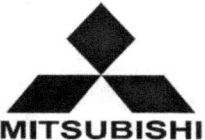

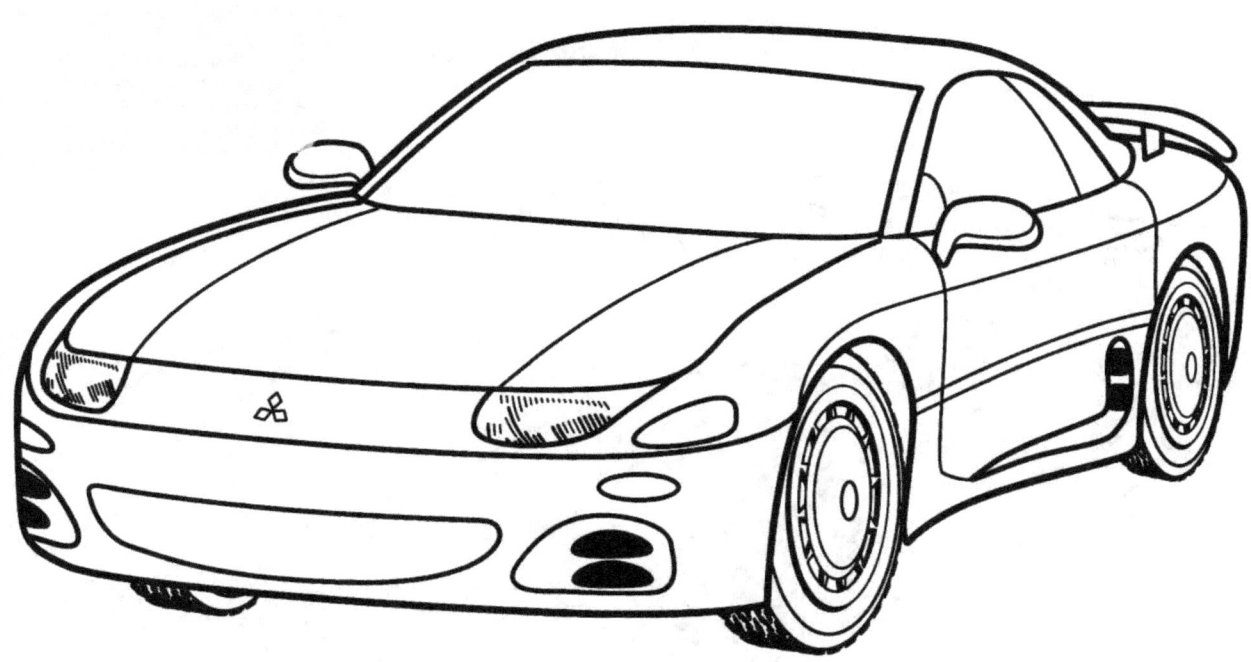

Acura - NSX
1991 - 2005
Made in Japan

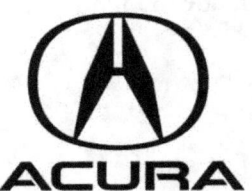

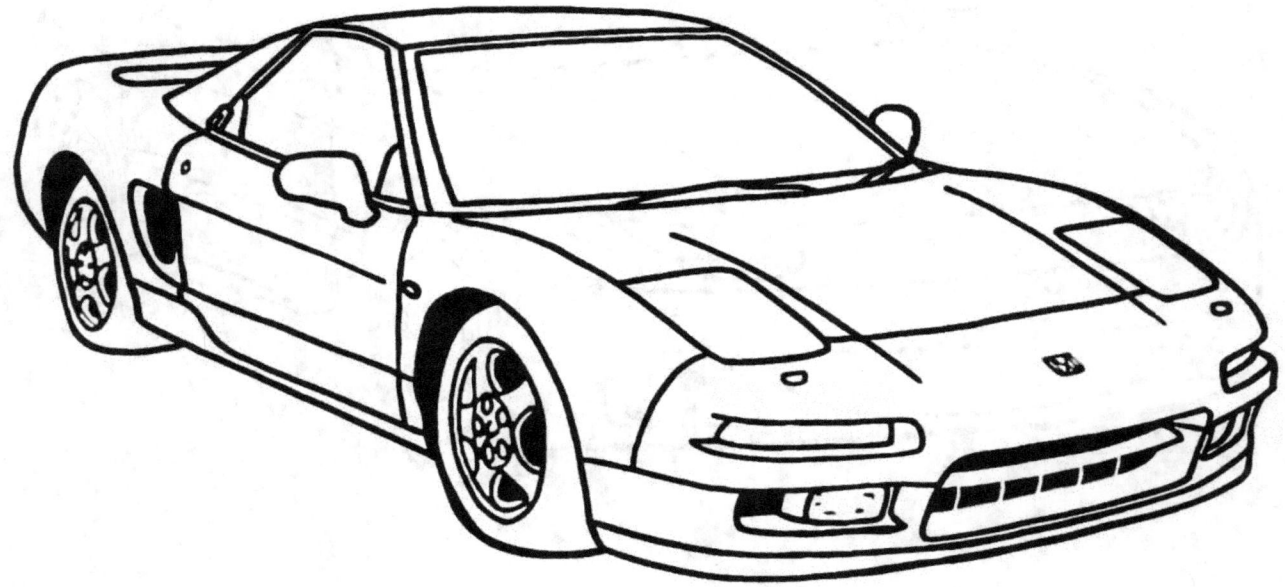

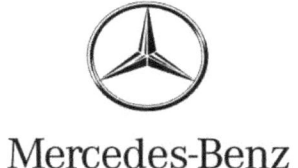
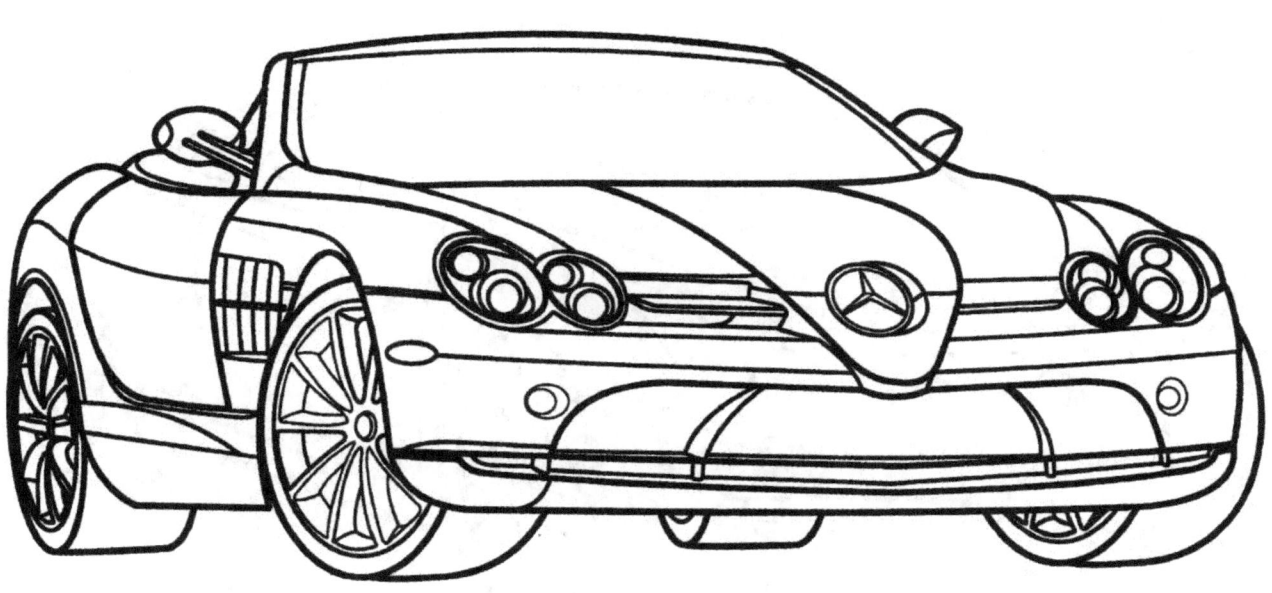

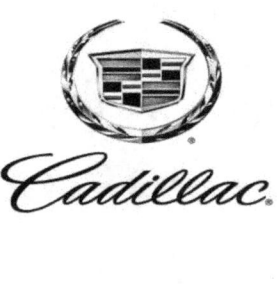
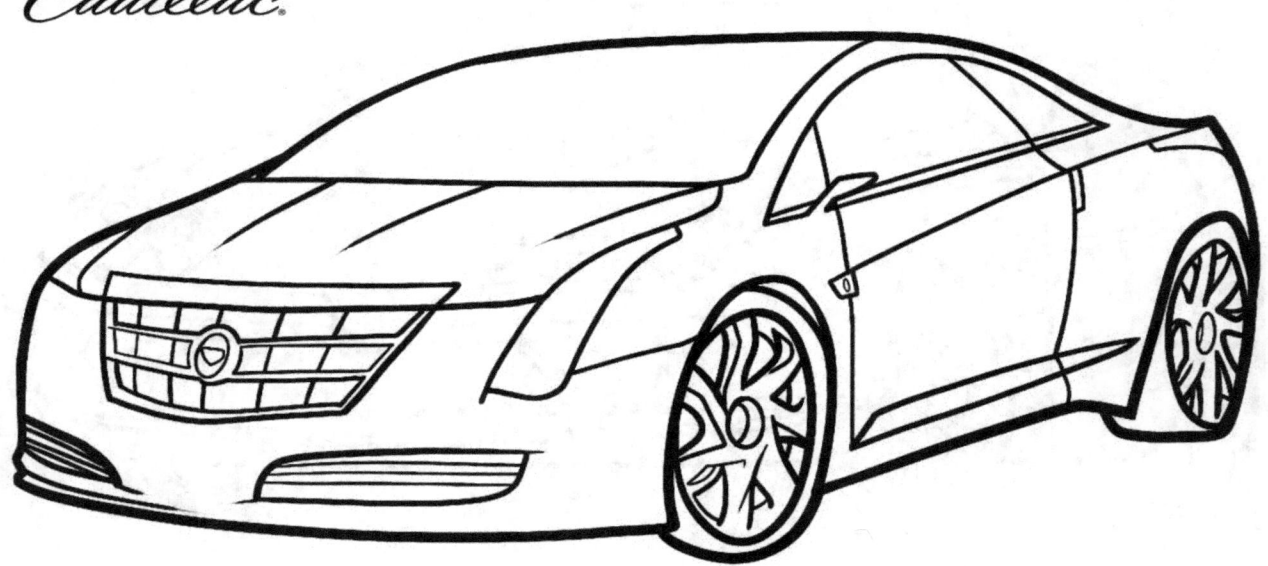

Gelandewagen - G-Class
1979 - Present Day
Made in Germany

Mercedes-Benz

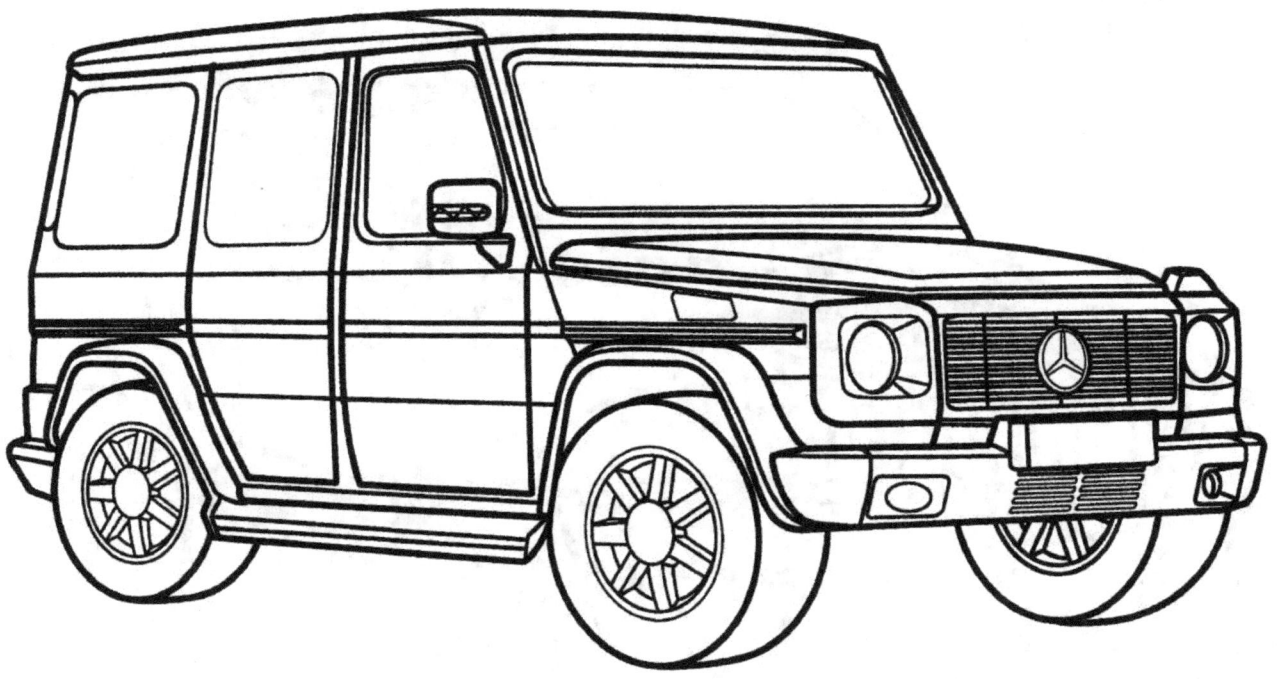

HUMMER
H3
2005 - 2010
Made in USA

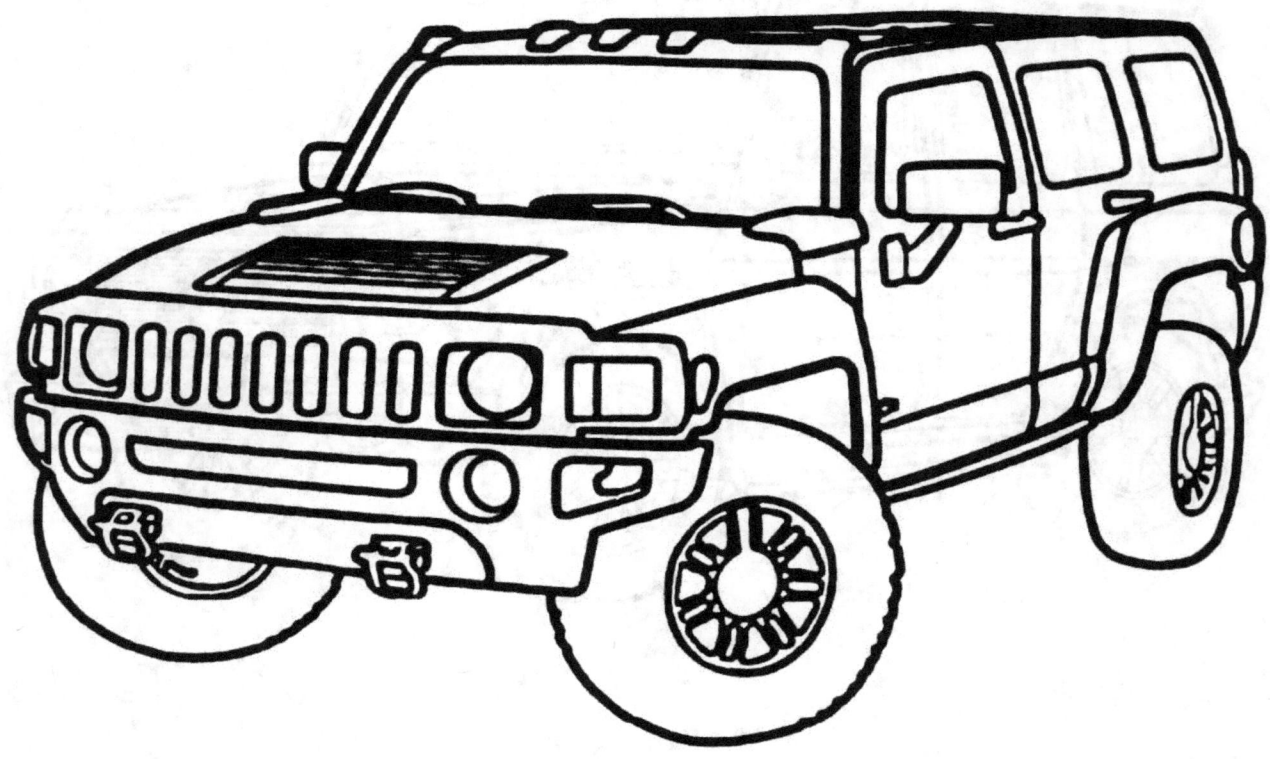

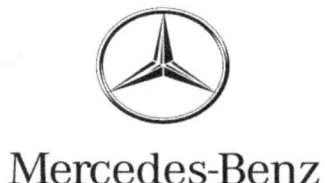
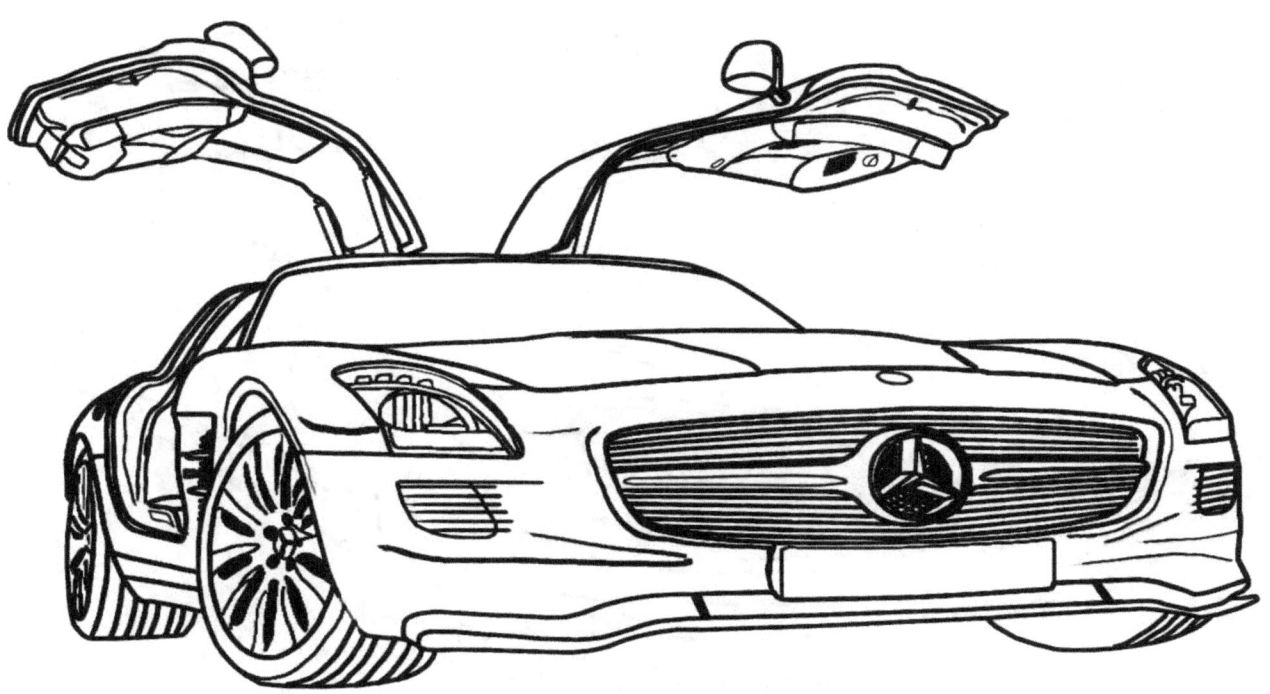

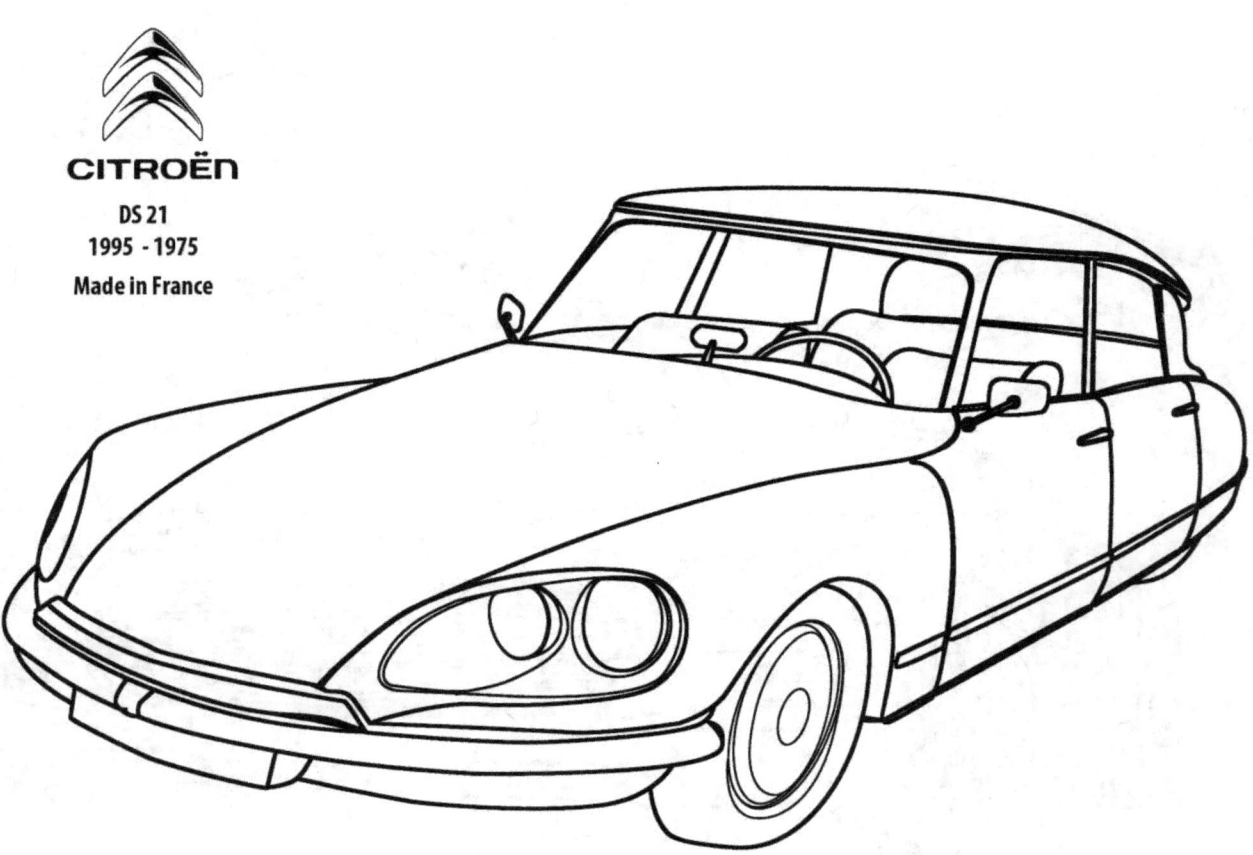

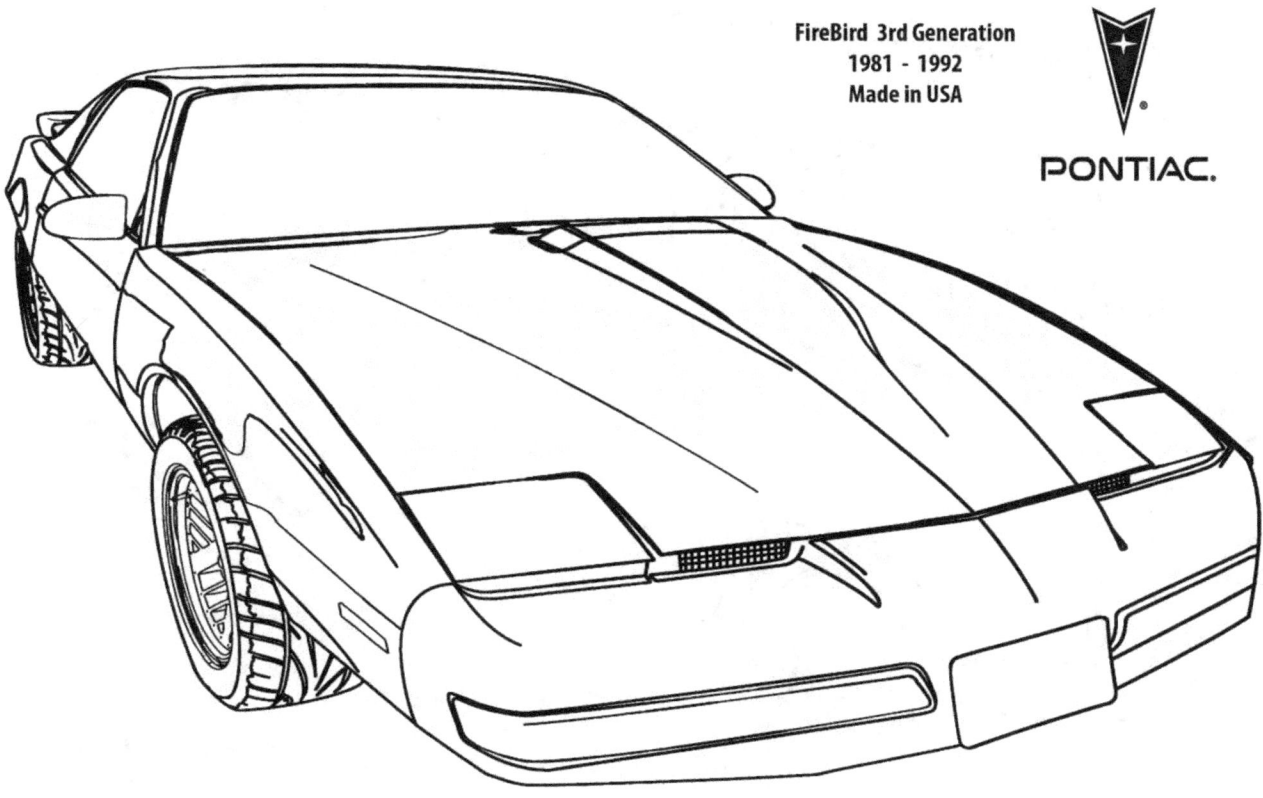

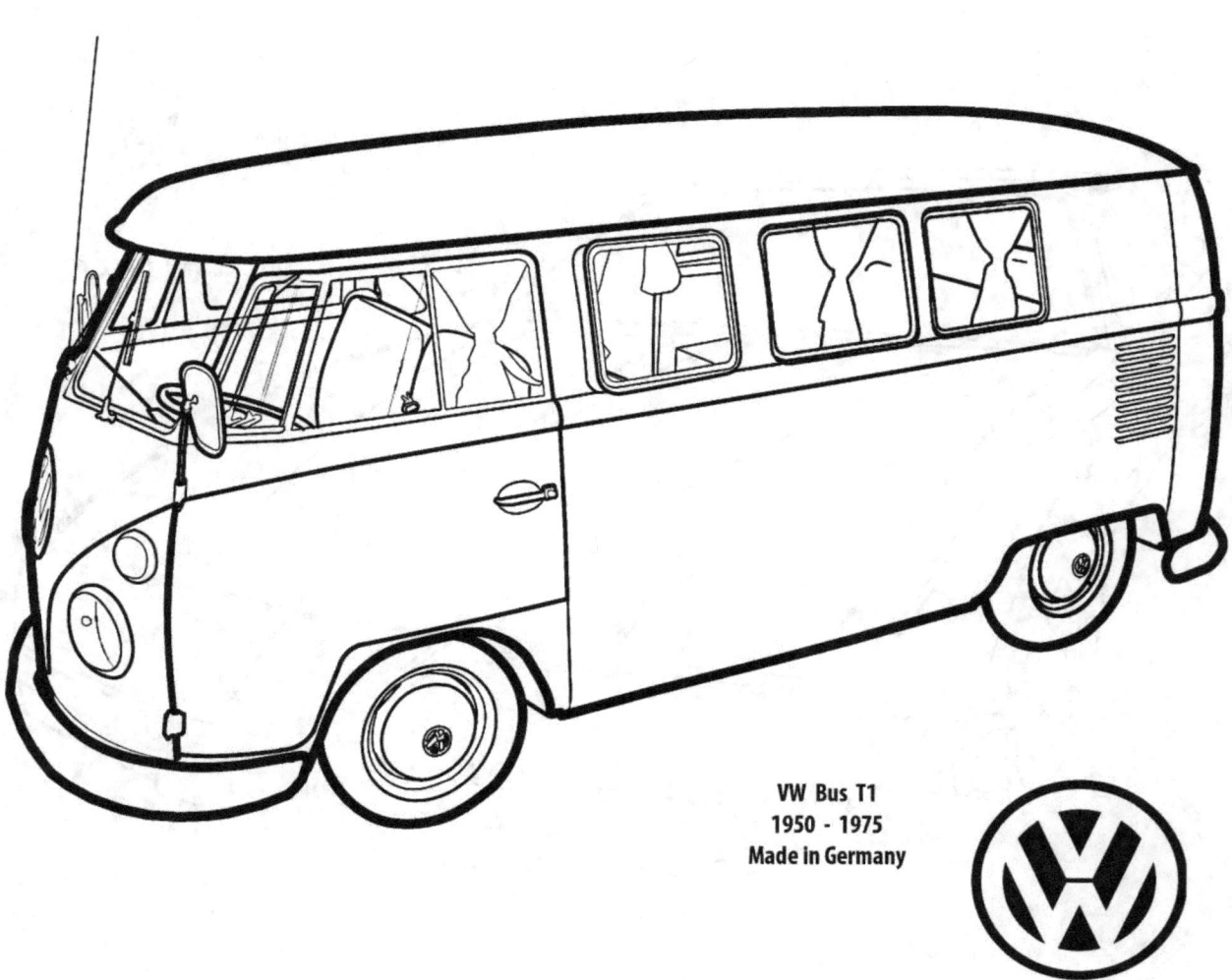

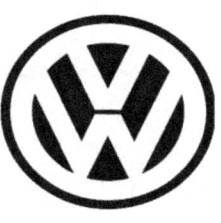

**VW Beatle
1938 - 2003
Made in Germany
(Still being assimbled in Mexico to this day)**

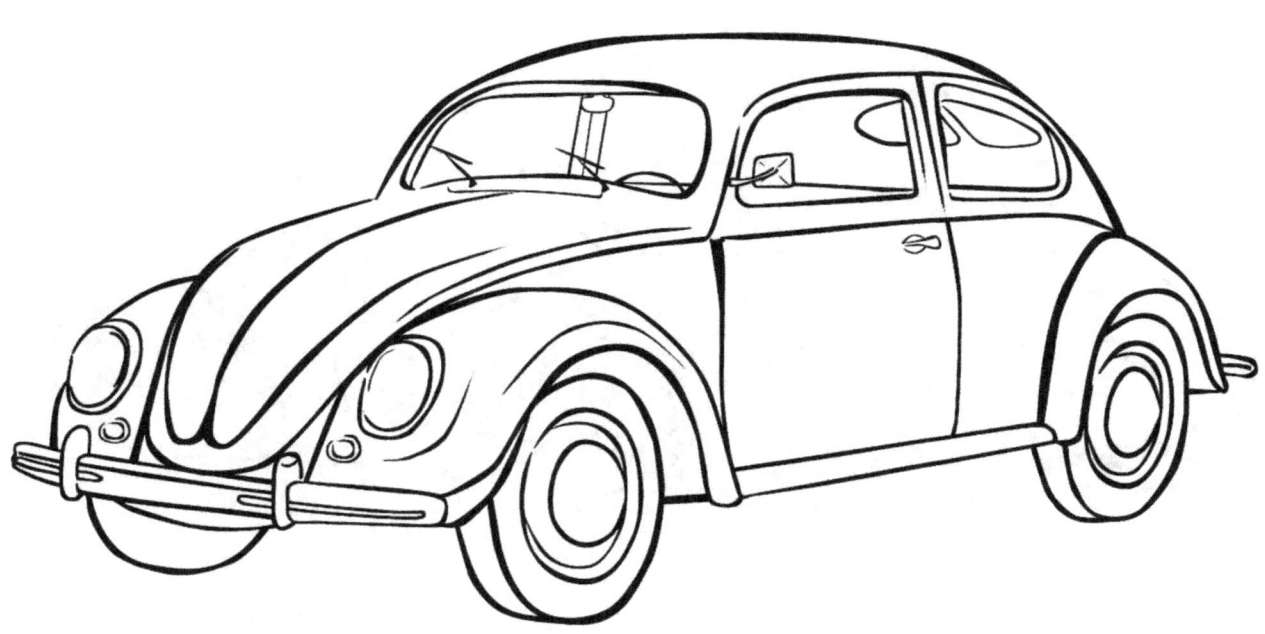

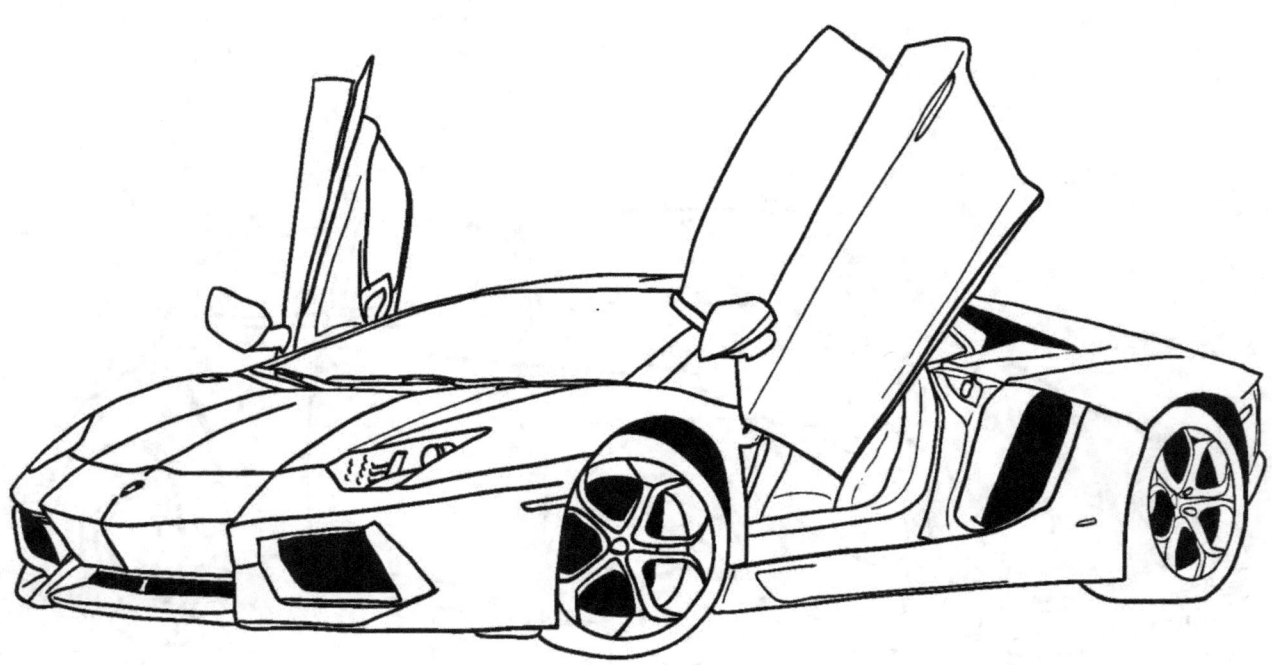

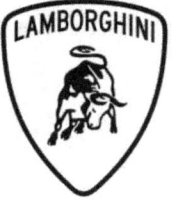

Aventador
2011 - Present day
Made in Italy

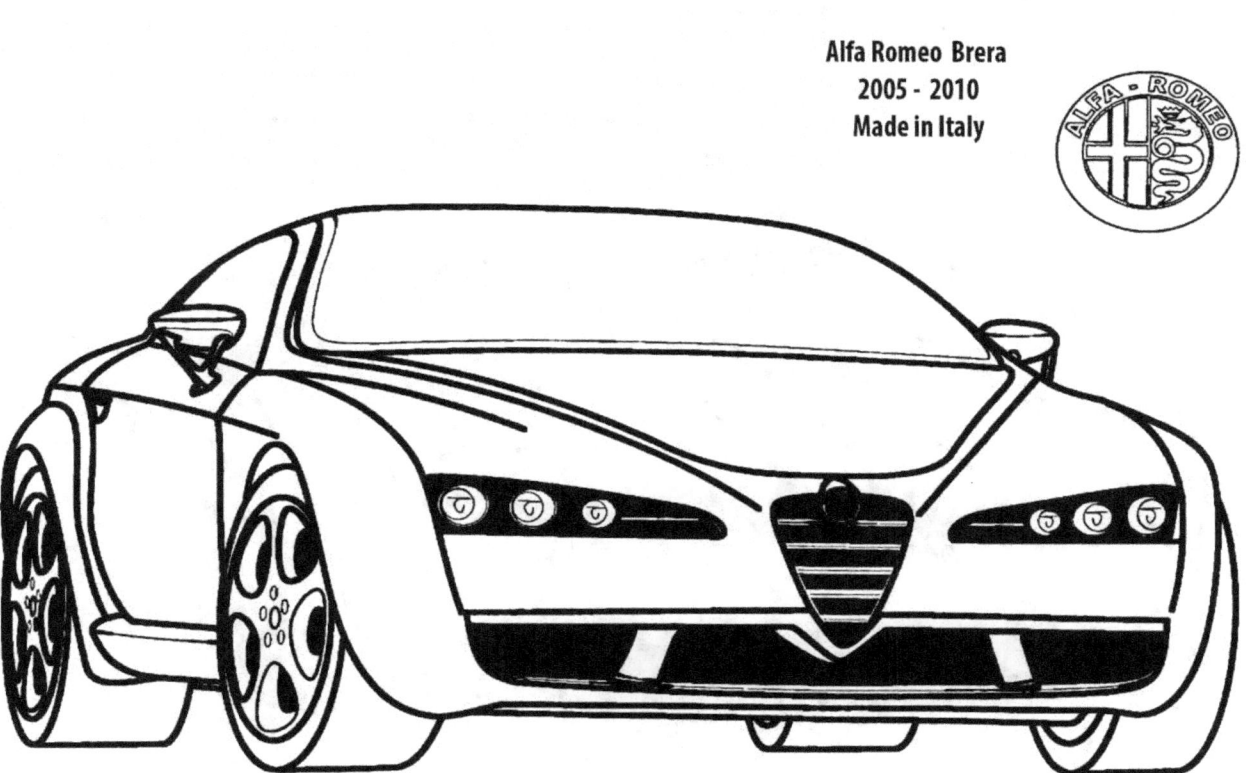

Alfa Romeo Brera
2005 - 2010
Made in Italy

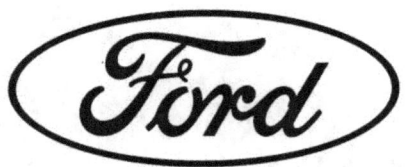

Ford GT
2004 -- 2006
Made in USA

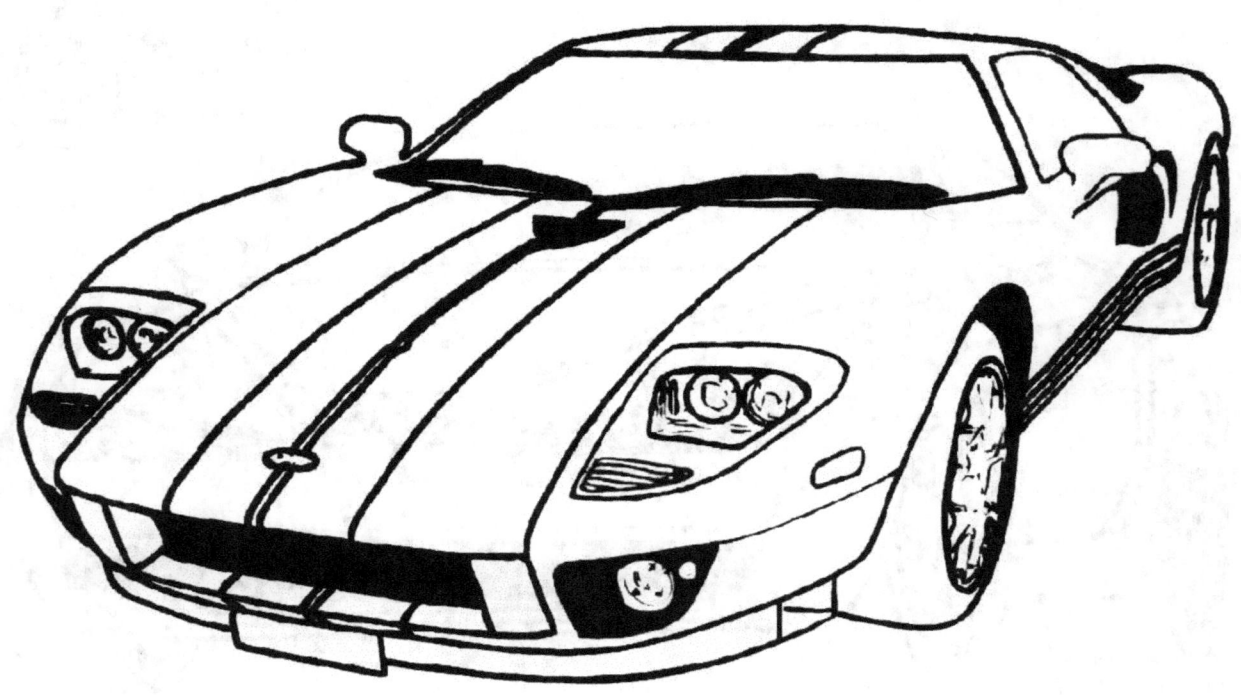

BMW - 640i
2003 - 2010
Made in Germany

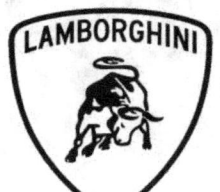

LAMBORGHINI - Diablo
1990 - 2001
Made in Italy

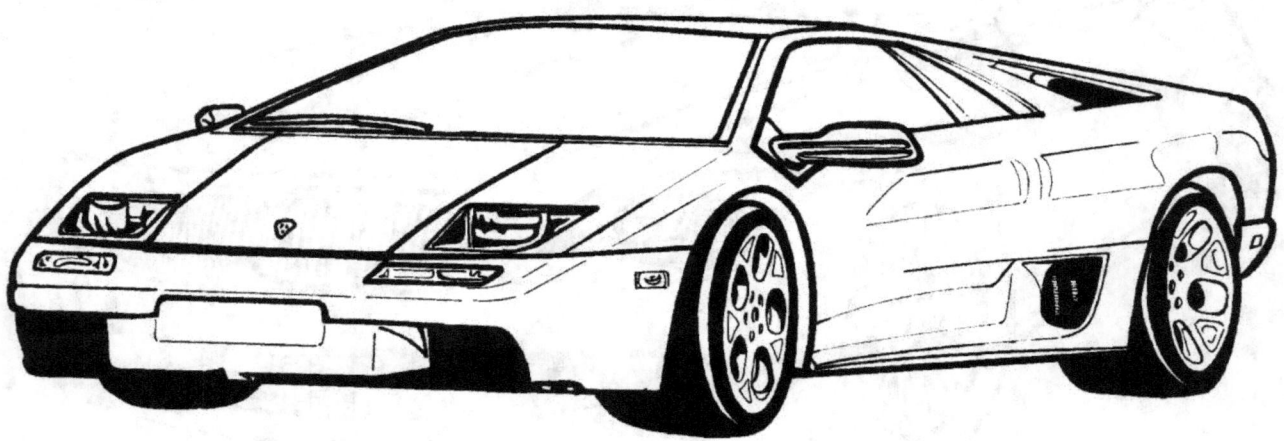

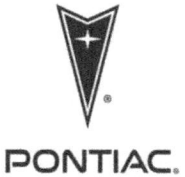

PONTIAC

Pontiac Trans Am WS
1998 - 2002
Made in USA

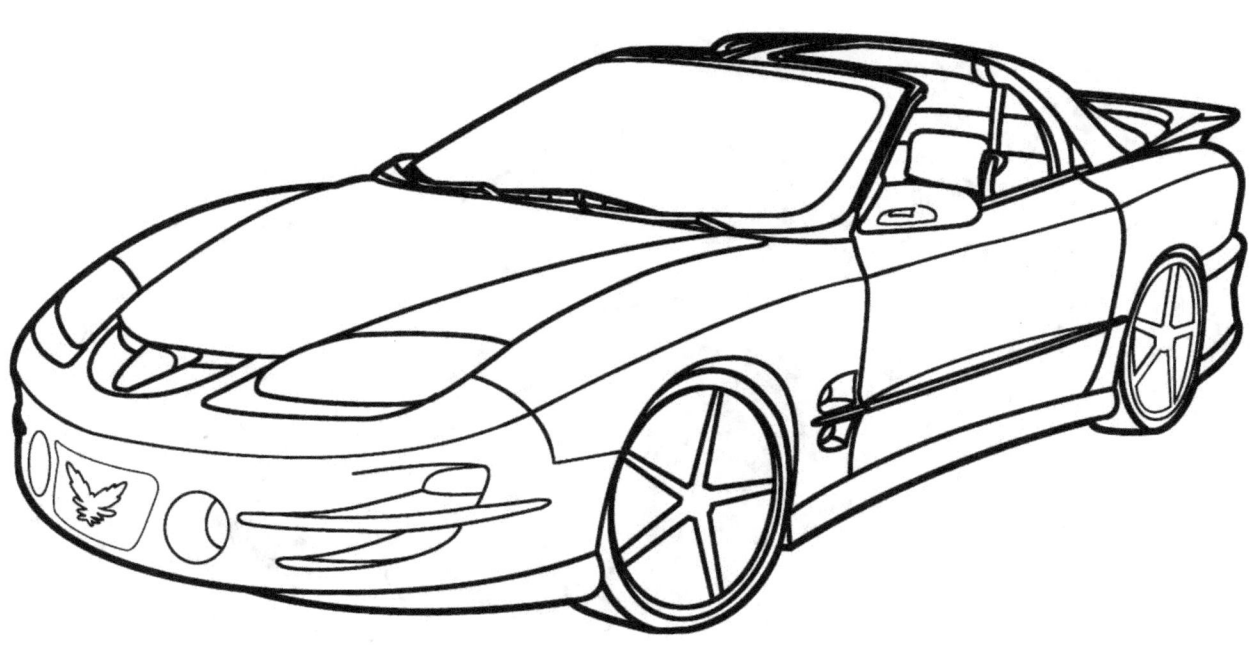

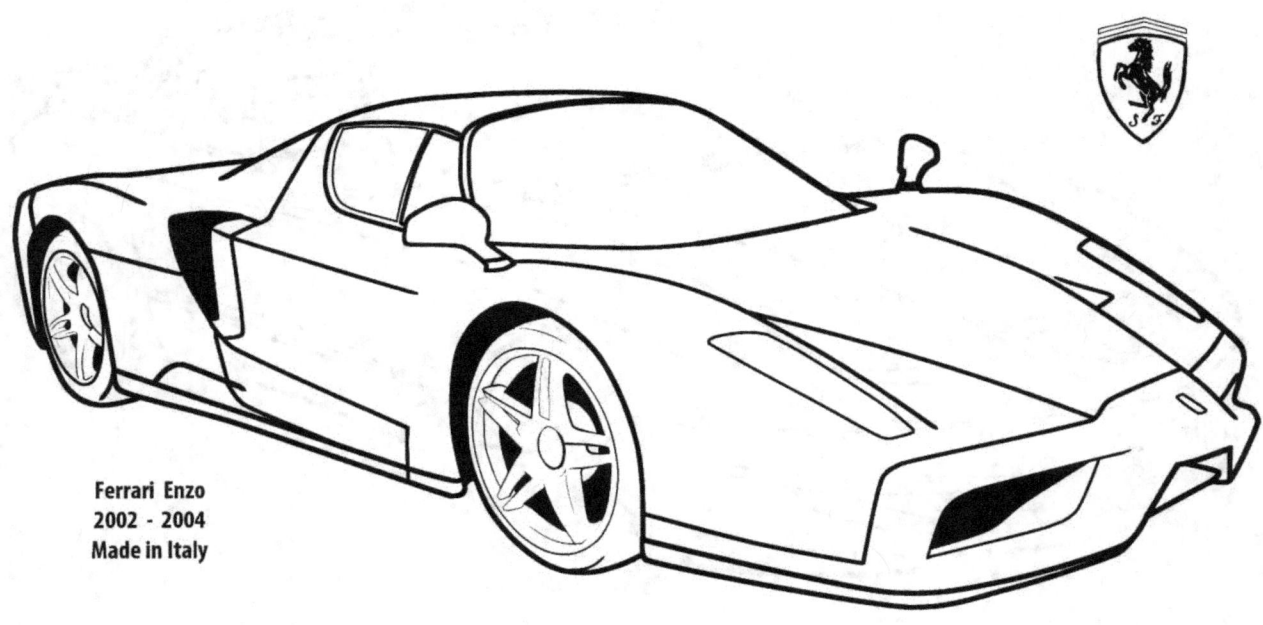

Ferrari Enzo
2002 - 2004
Made in Italy

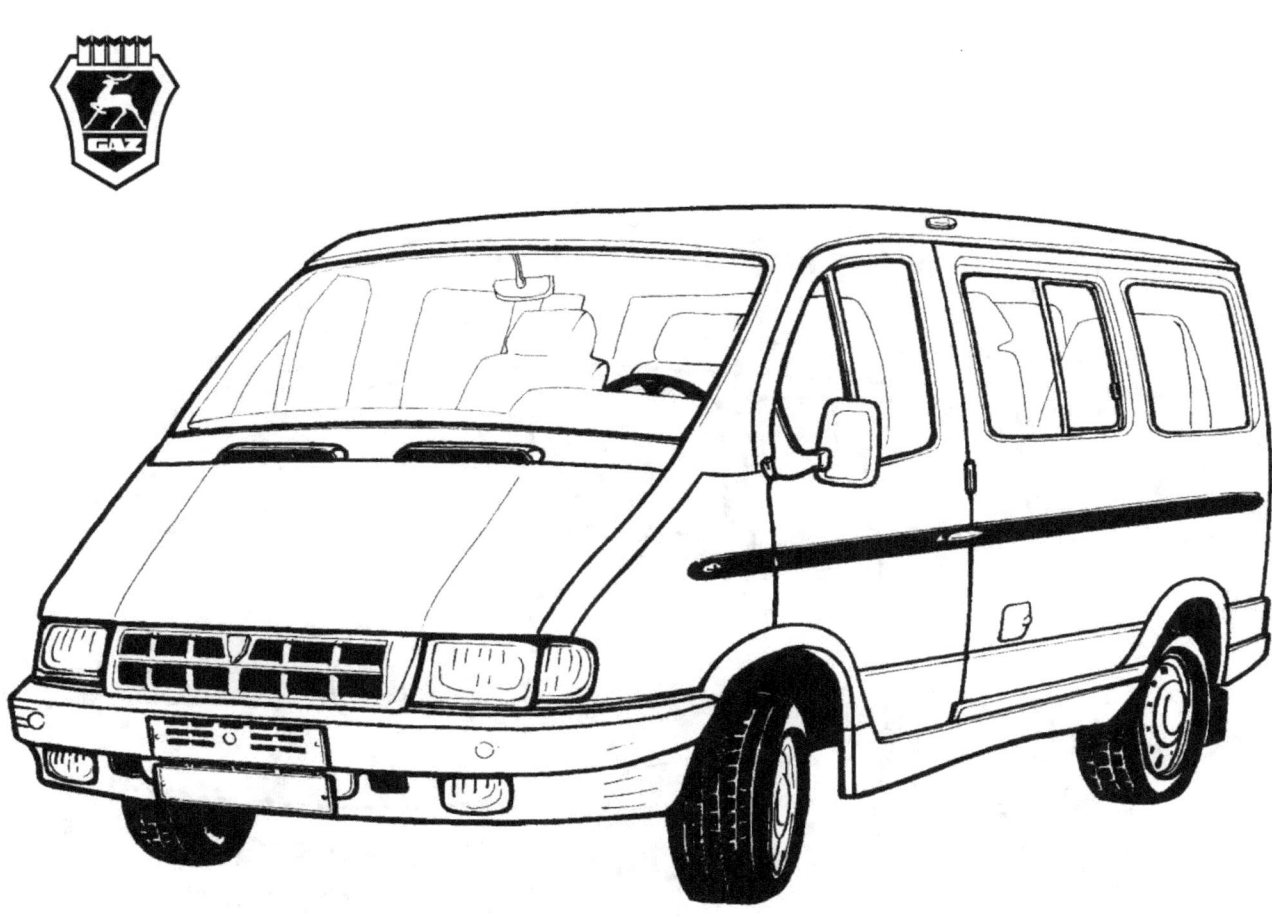

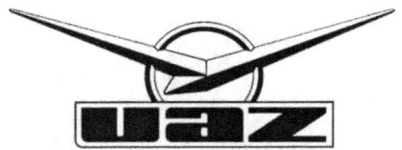

UAZ - 452
1965 - Present Day
Made in Russia

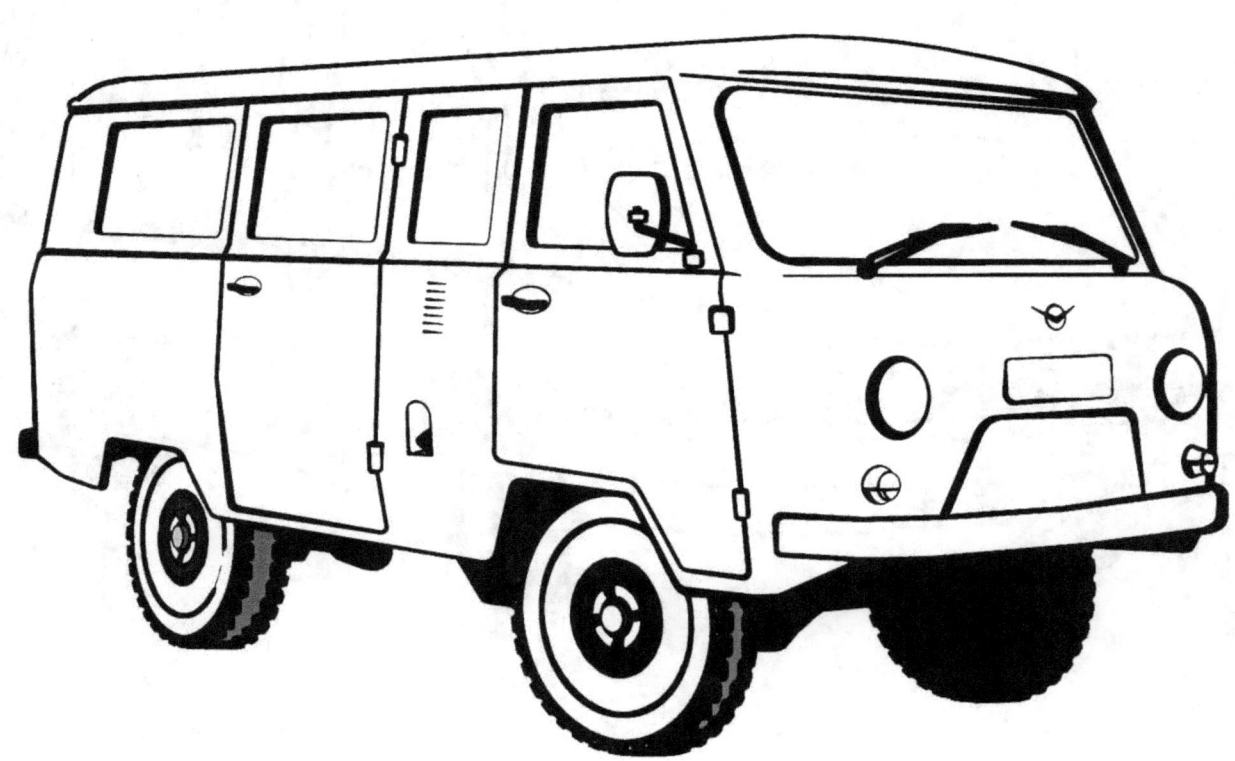

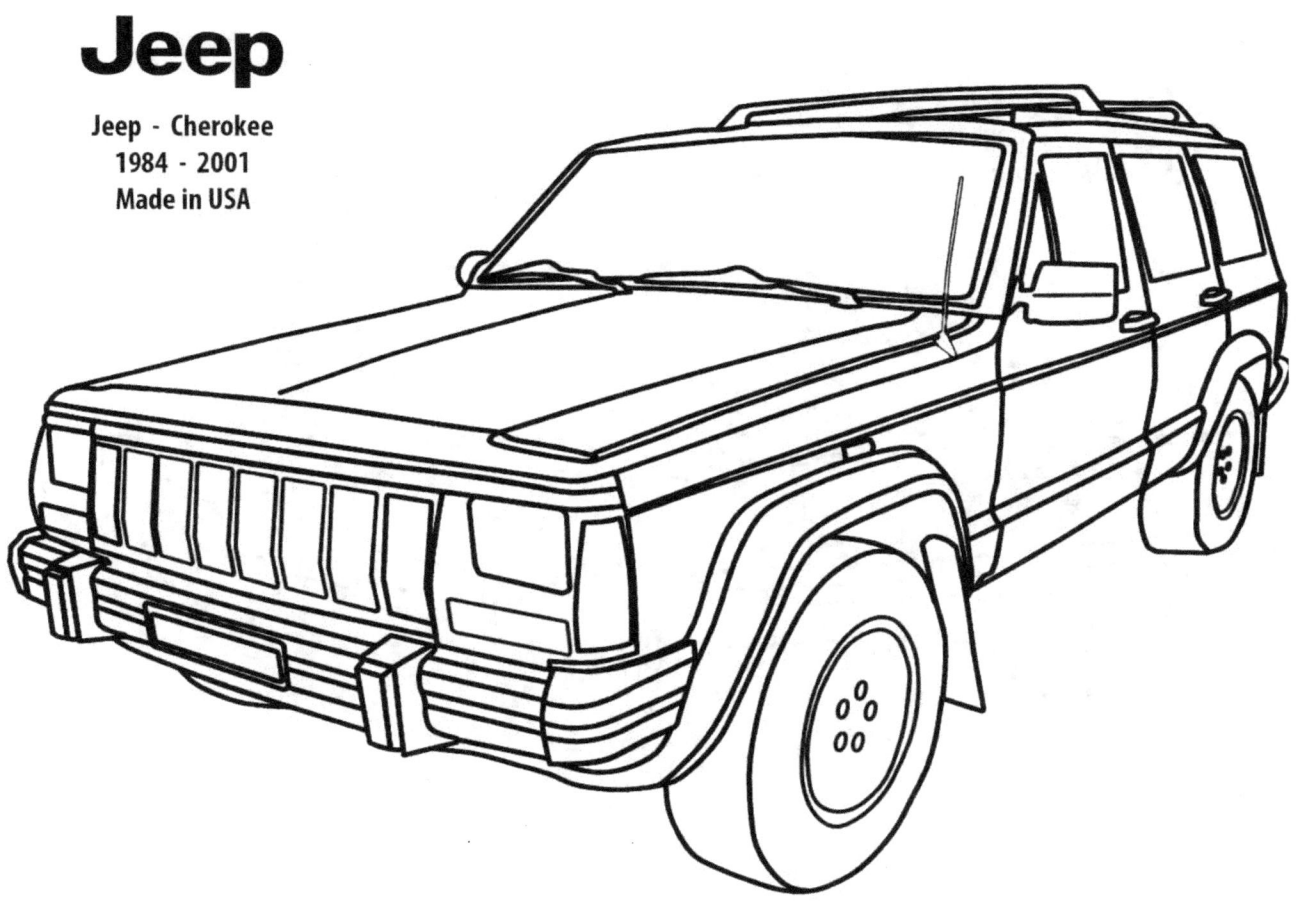

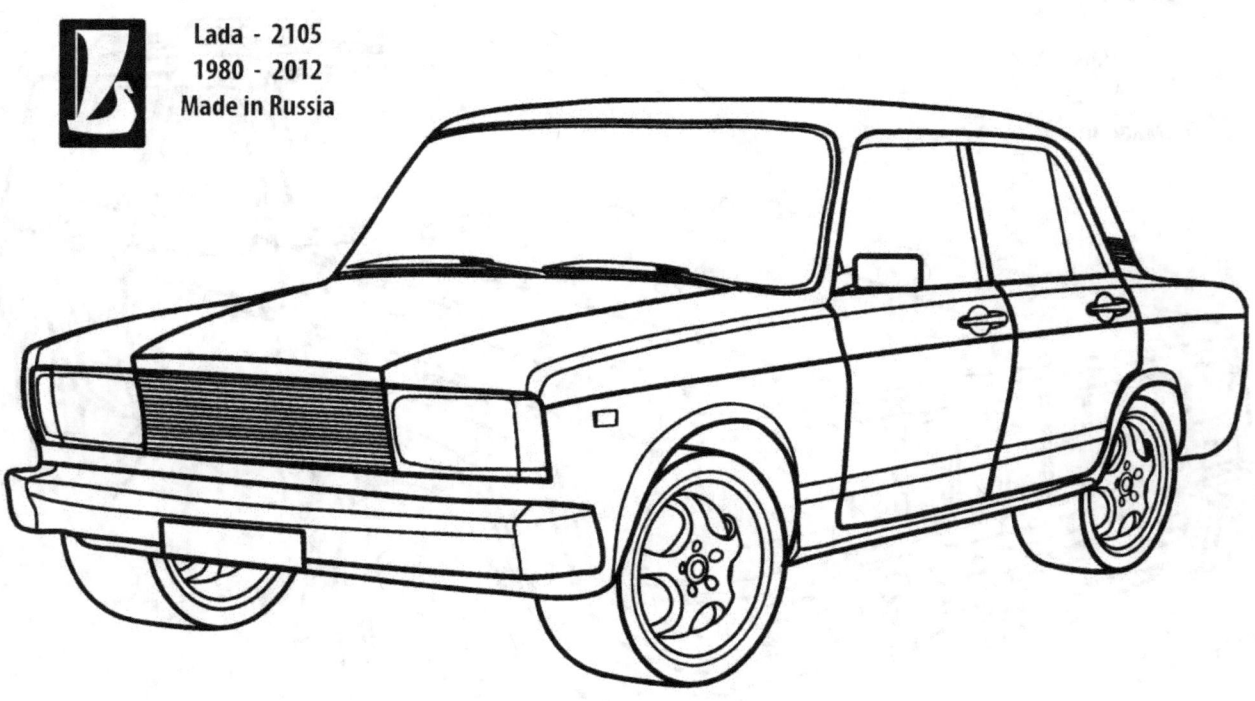

Lada - 2105
1980 - 2012
Made in Russia

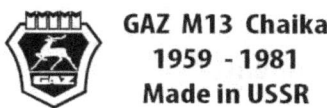

GAZ M13 Chaika
1959 - 1981
Made in USSR

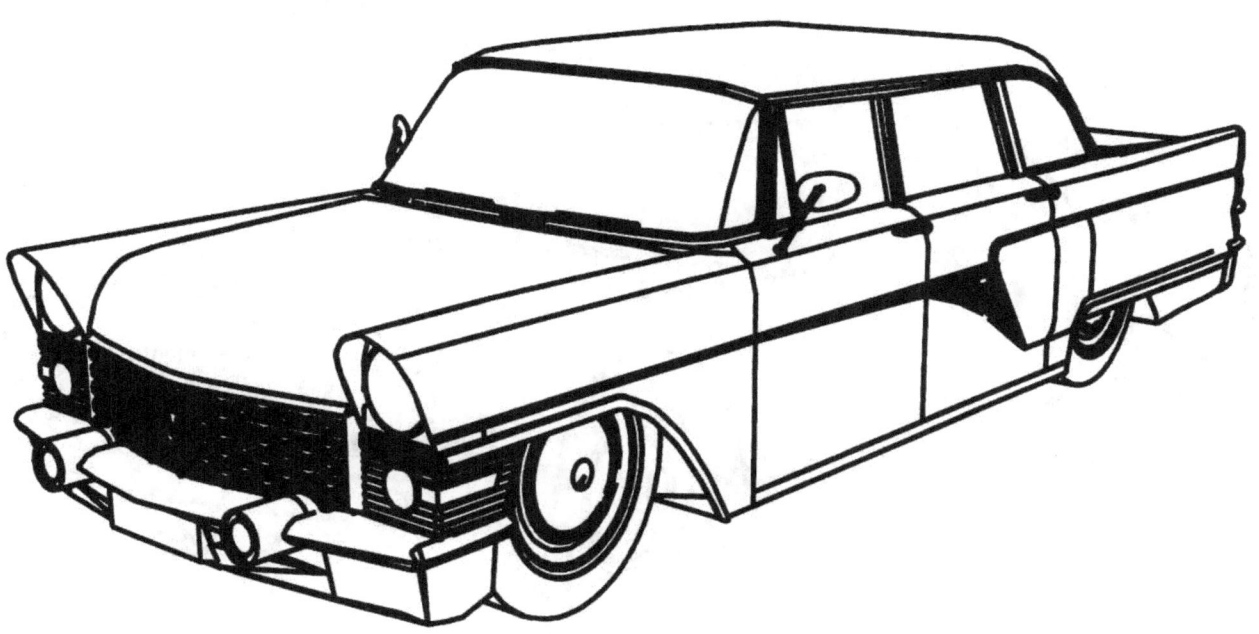

Lincoln Continental
1961 - 1969
Made in USA

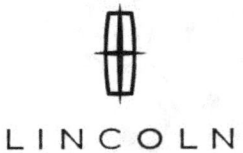

LINCOLN

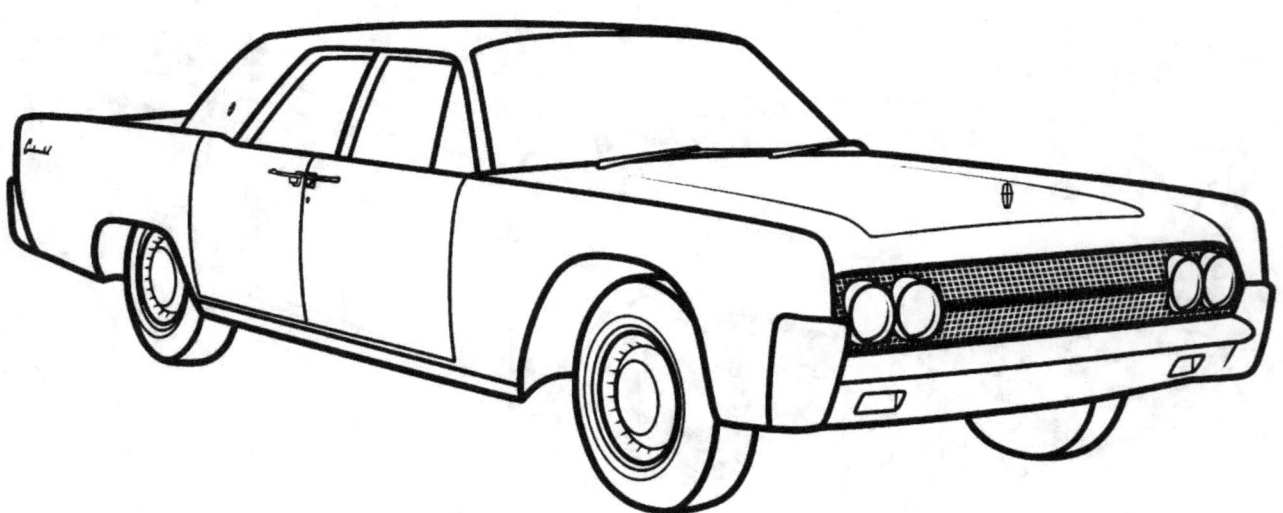

Audi R8
2006 - 2015
Made in Germany

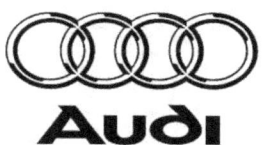

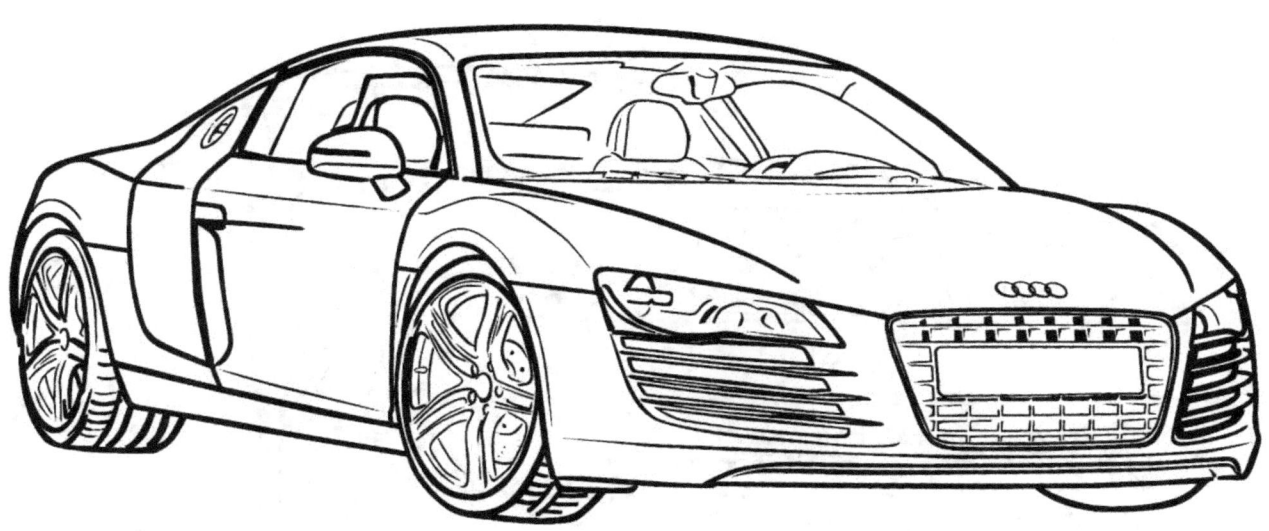

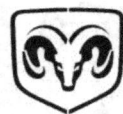

Dodge Challenger
2008 - Present Day
Made in USA

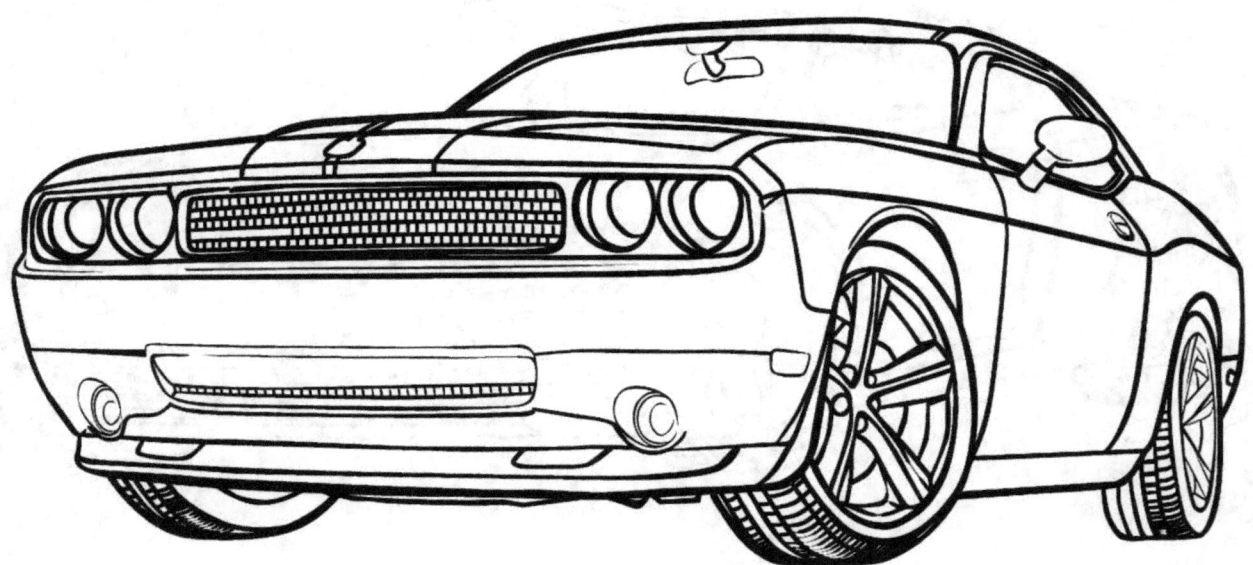

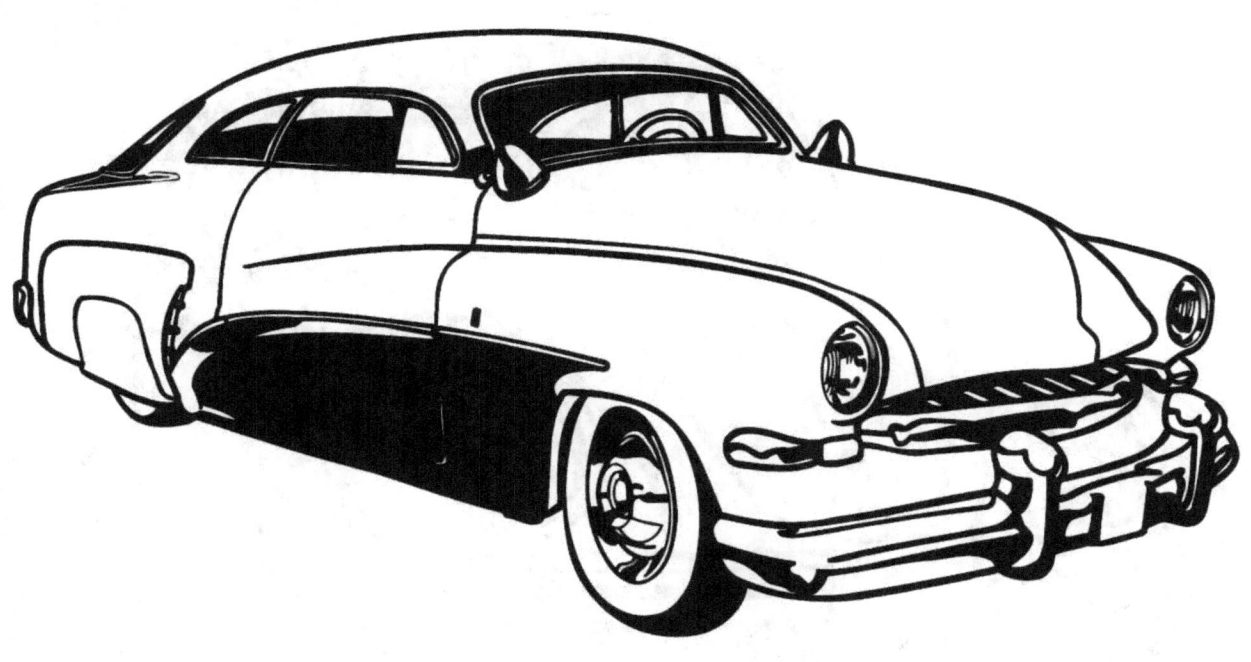

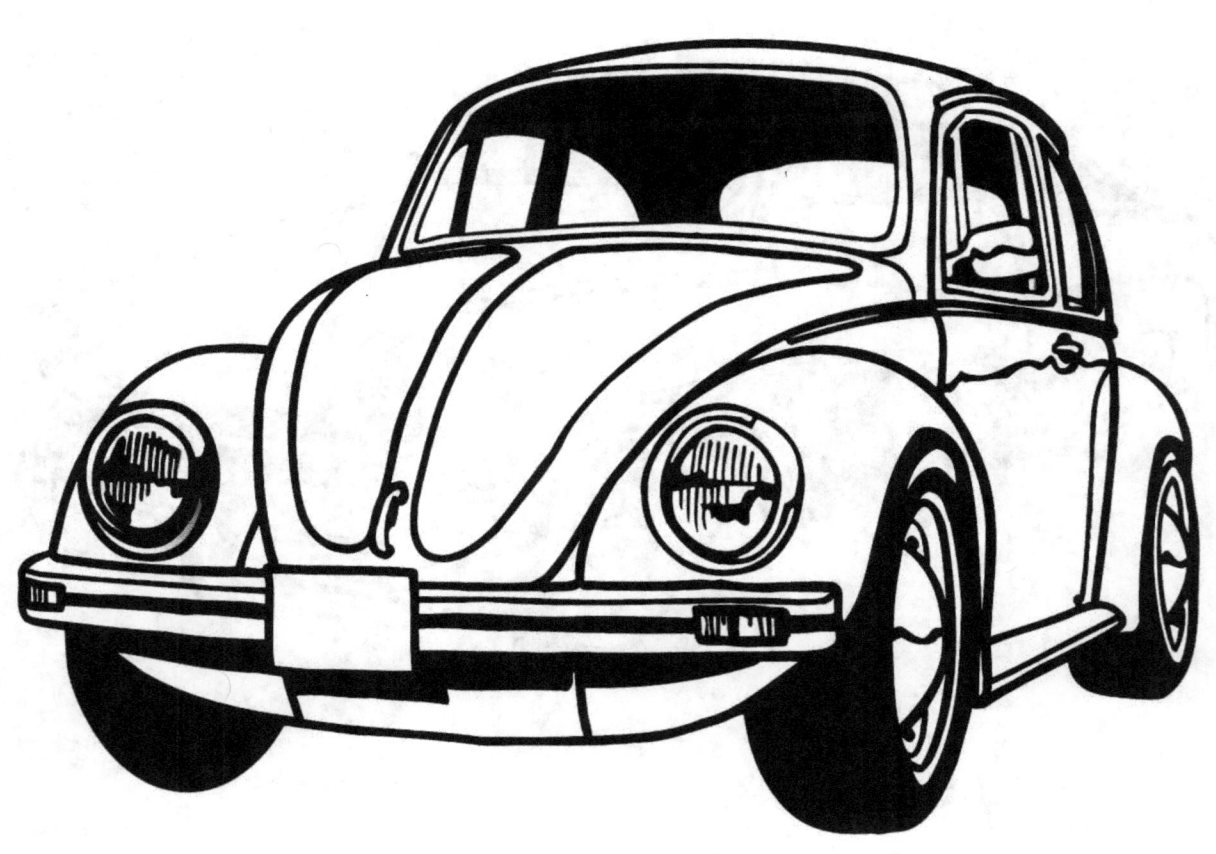

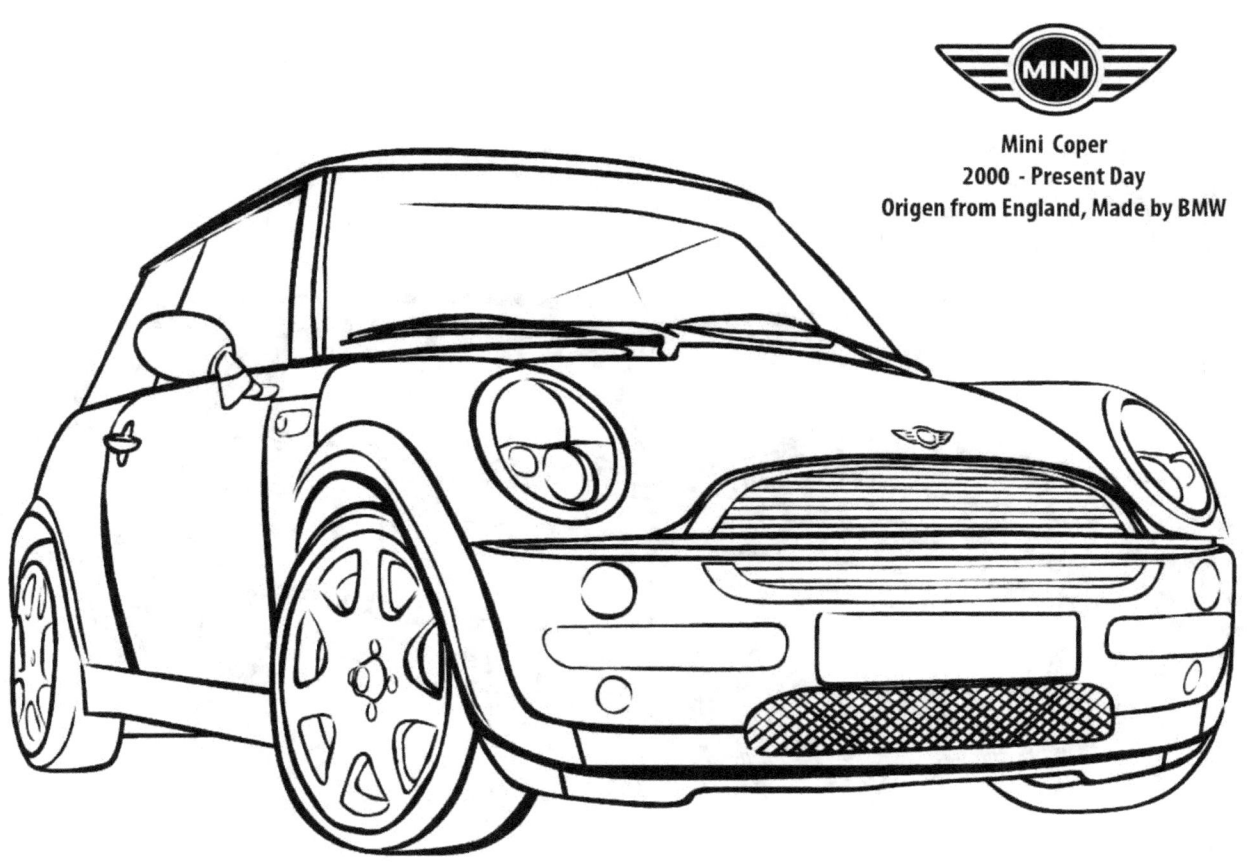

Mini Coper
2000 - Present Day
Origen from England, Made by BMW

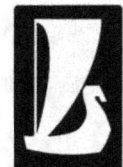

LADA VAZ - 2104
1984 - 2012
Made in Russia
Export Version

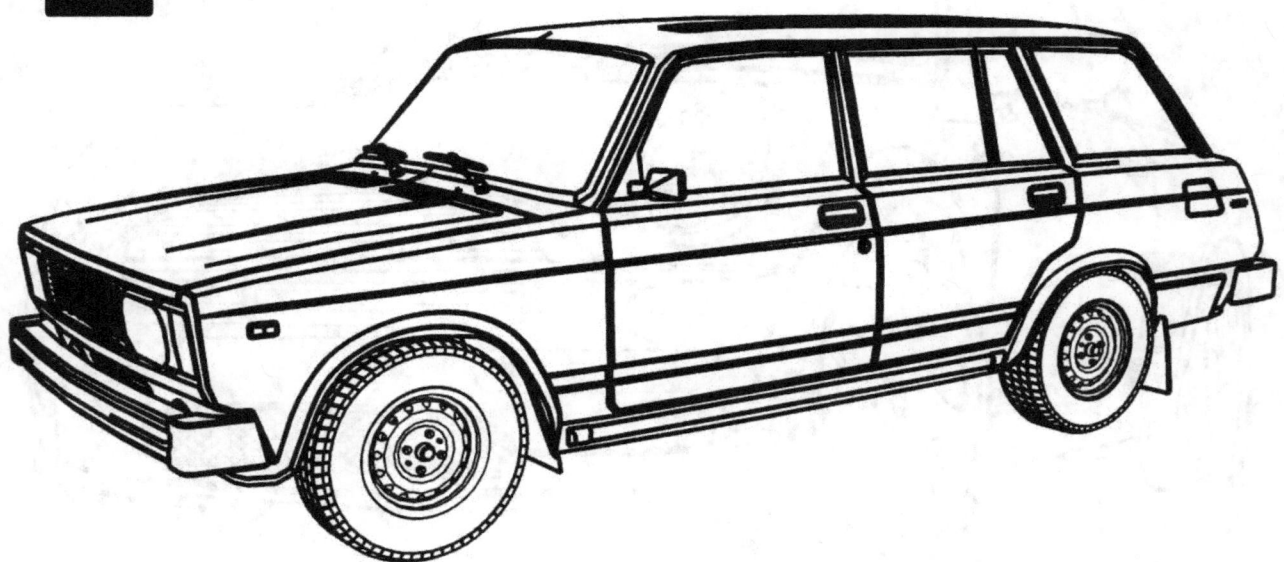

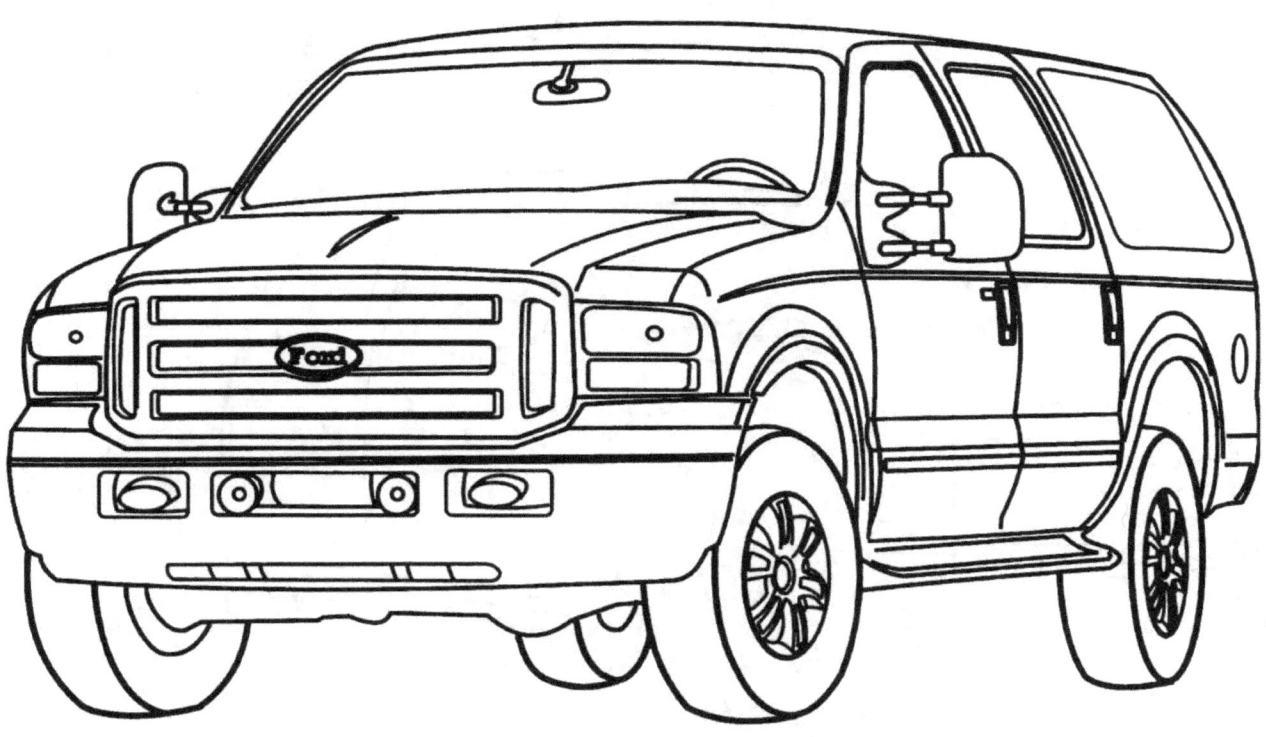

Ford Excursion
2000 - 2004
Made in USA

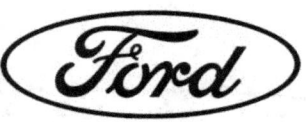

Ford F150
2015 - Present Day
Made in USA

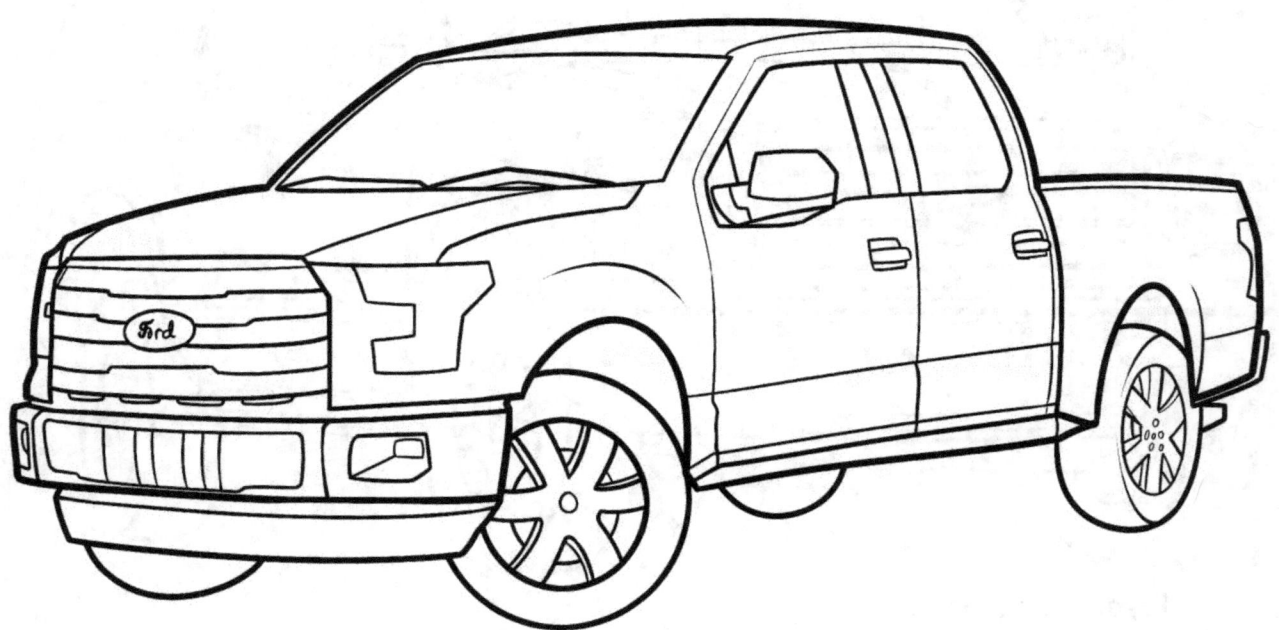

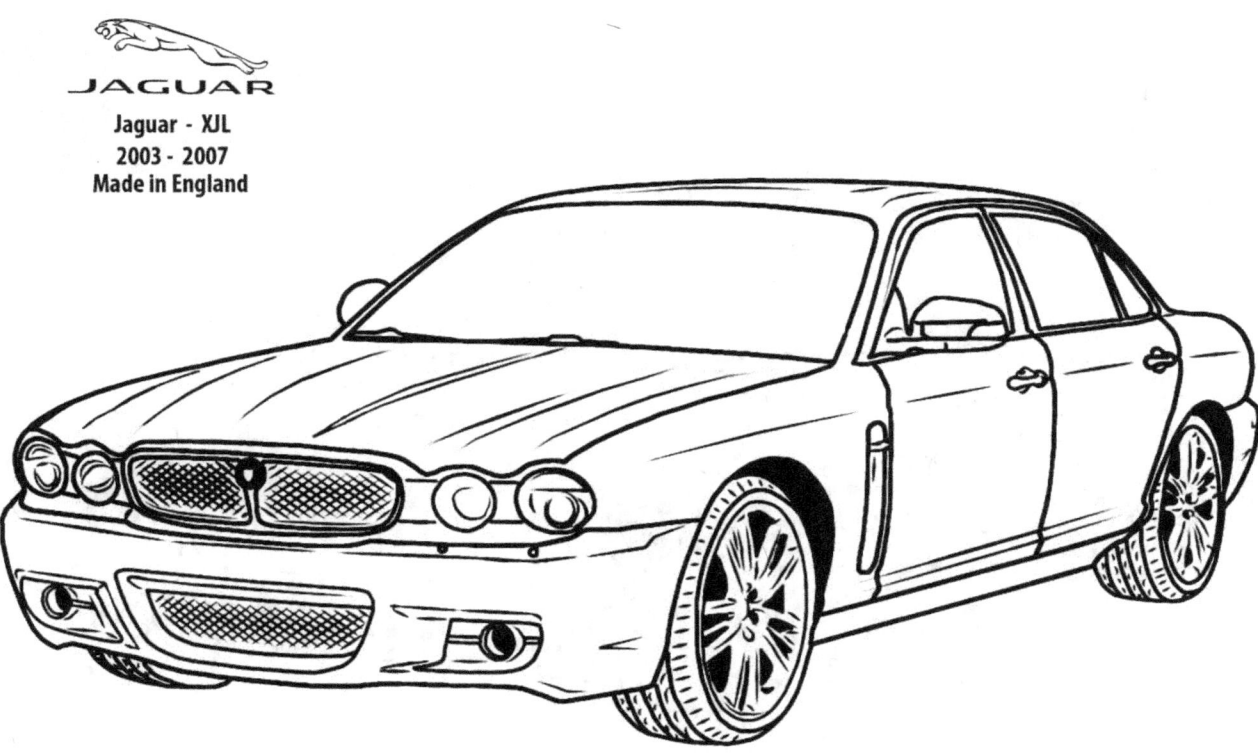

Jaguar - XJL
2003 - 2007
Made in England

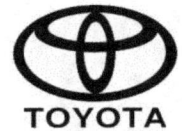

Toyota Tundra
1999 - Present Day
Made in Japan

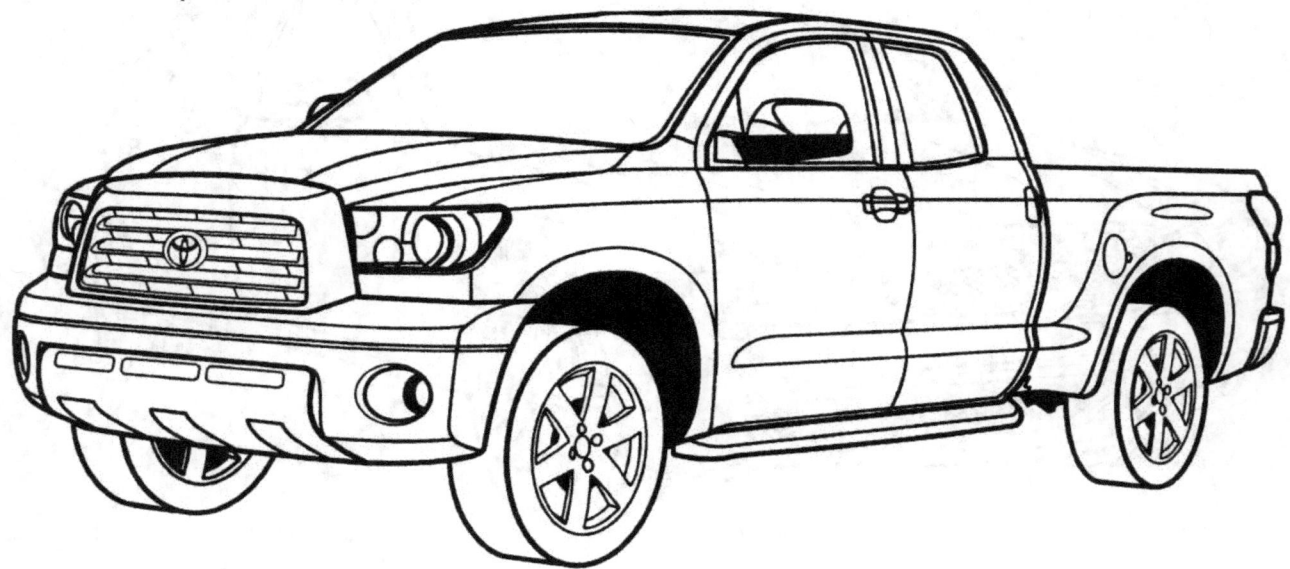

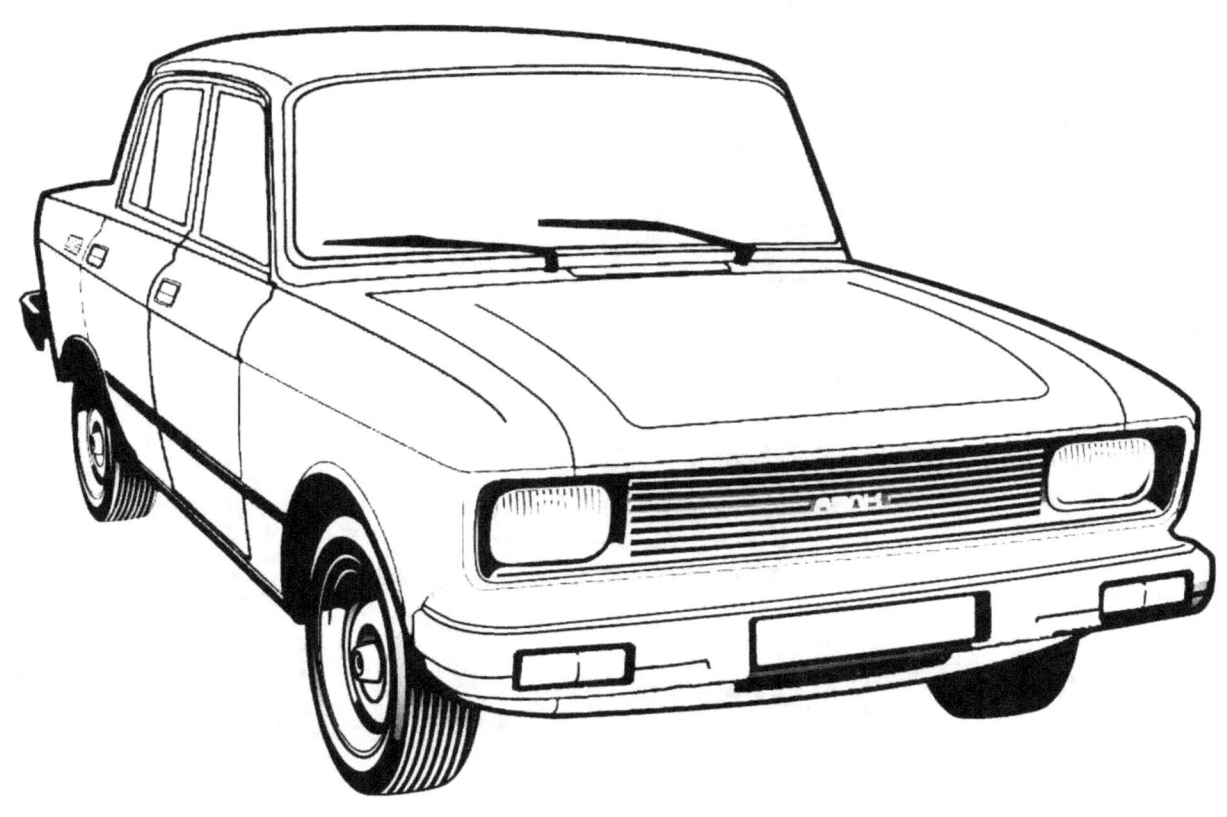

Moskvich 412
1967 - 2001
Made in USSR / Russia

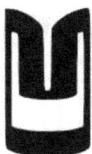

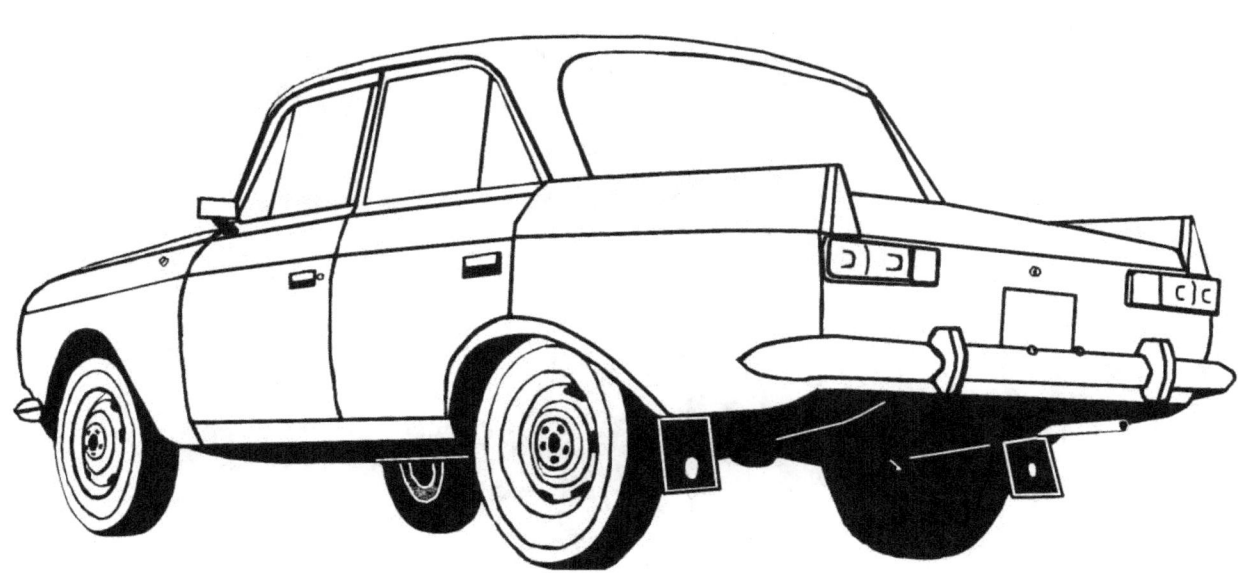

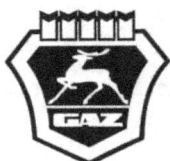

GAZ M21 Volga
1956-1970
Made in USSR (Russia)

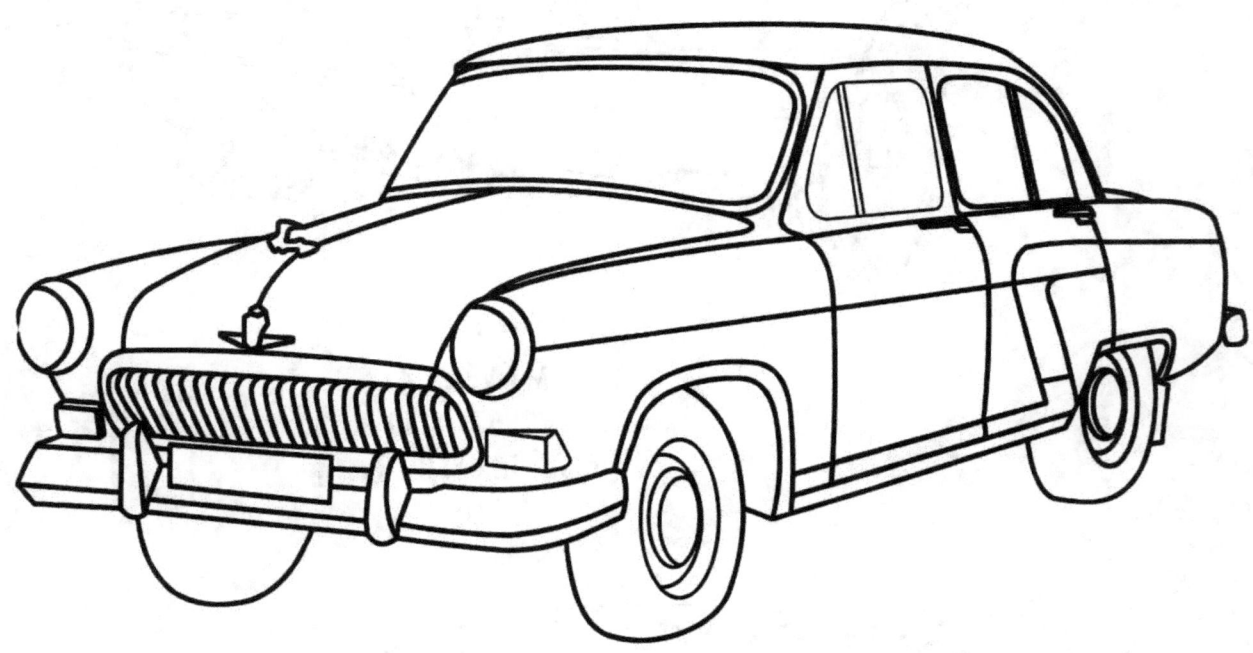

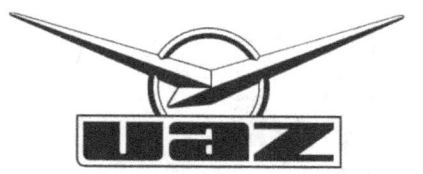

UAZ 469
1971-Present day
Made in USR (Russia)

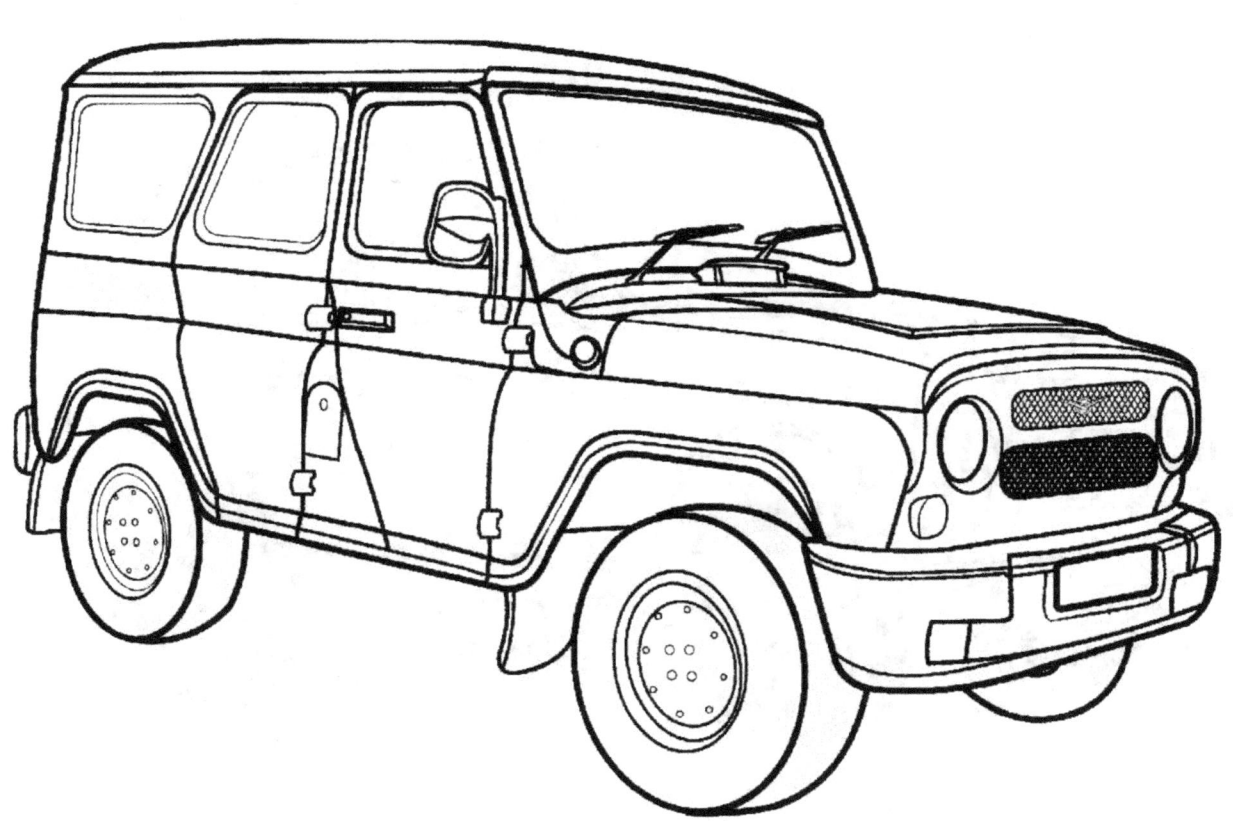

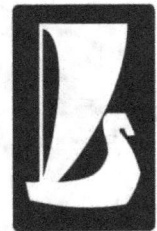

Lada AvtoVaz Niva 4x4
1977-Present day
Made in USSR (Russia)

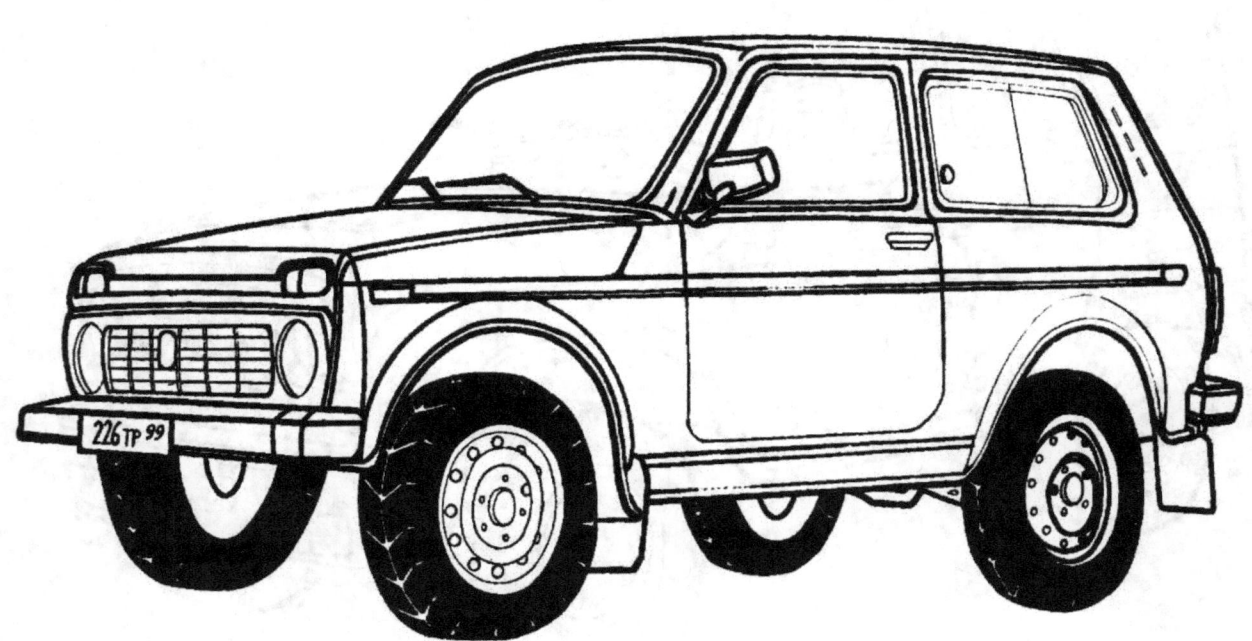

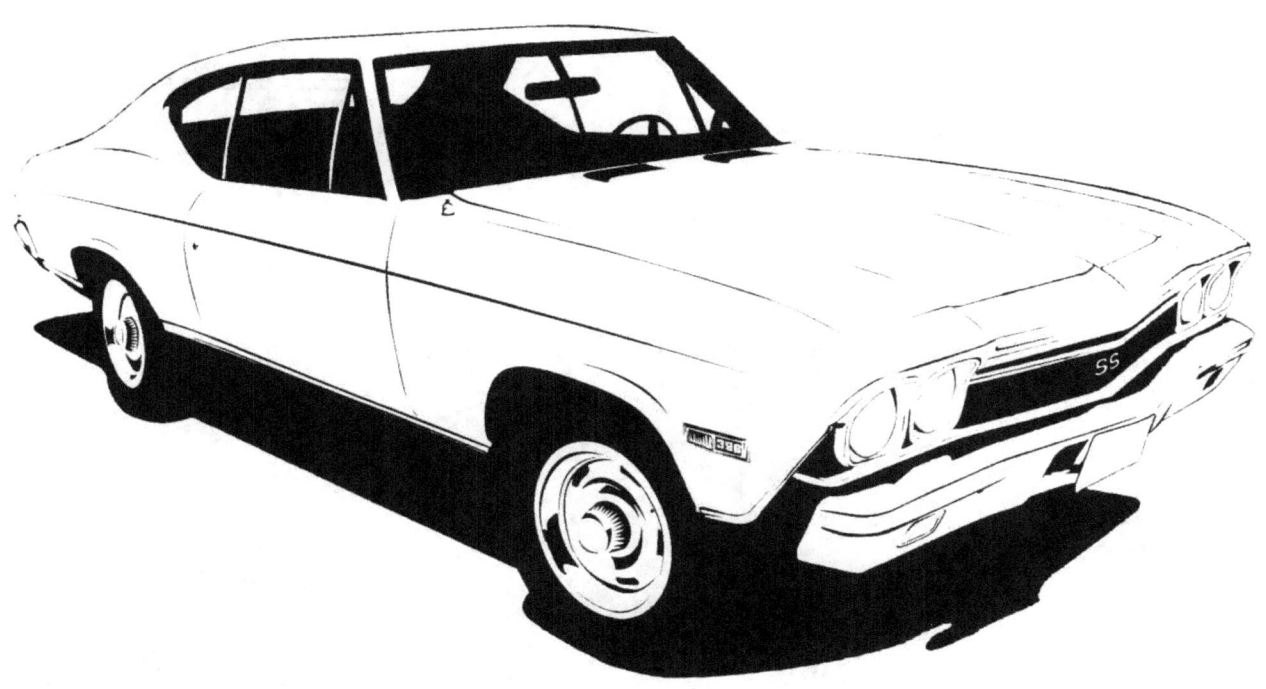

1968 Chevrolet Chevelle SS

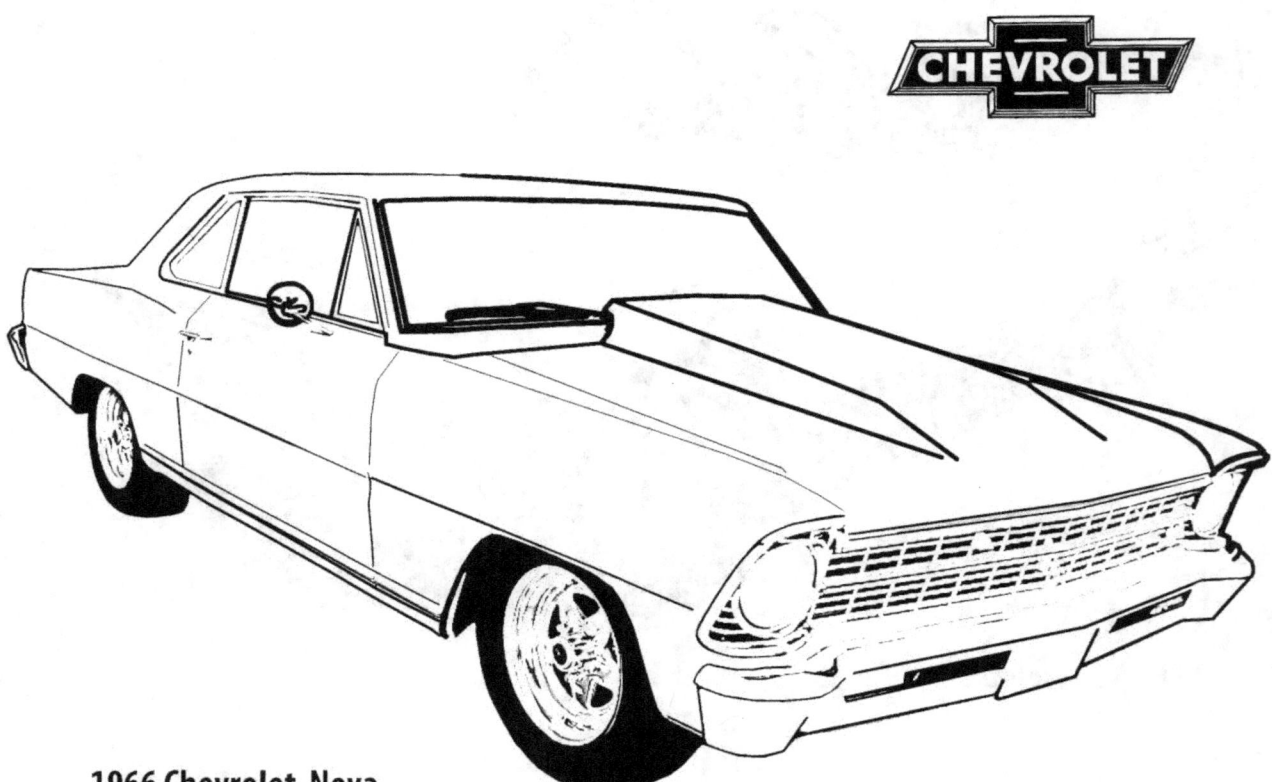

1966 Chevrolet Nova

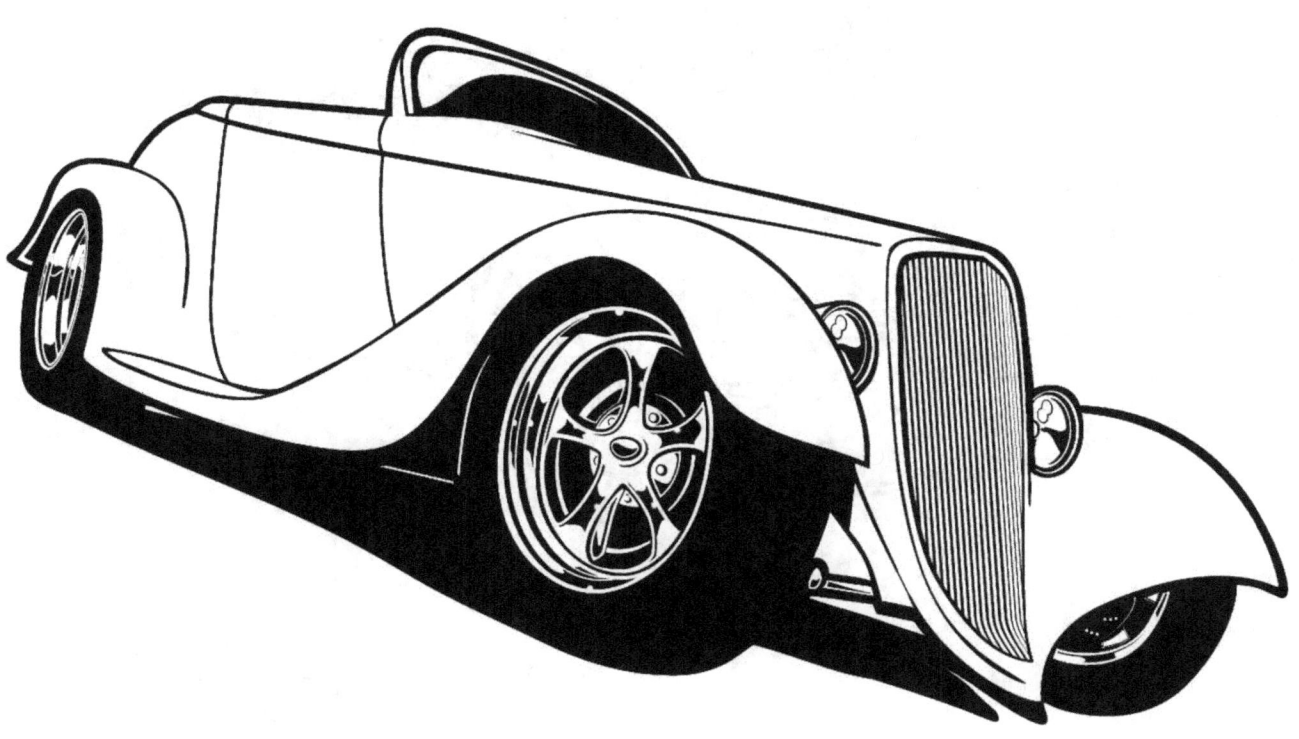

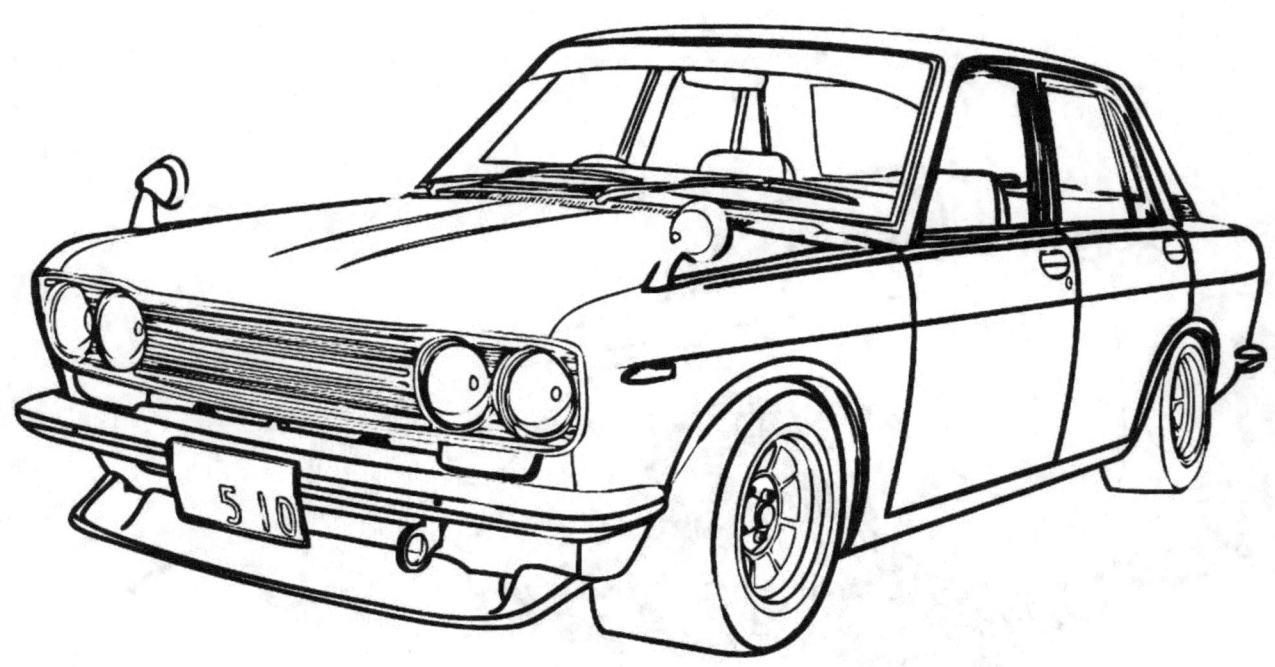

Datsun 510
1967 - 1973
Made in Japan

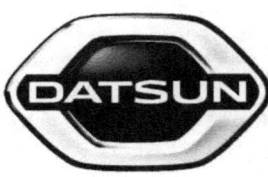

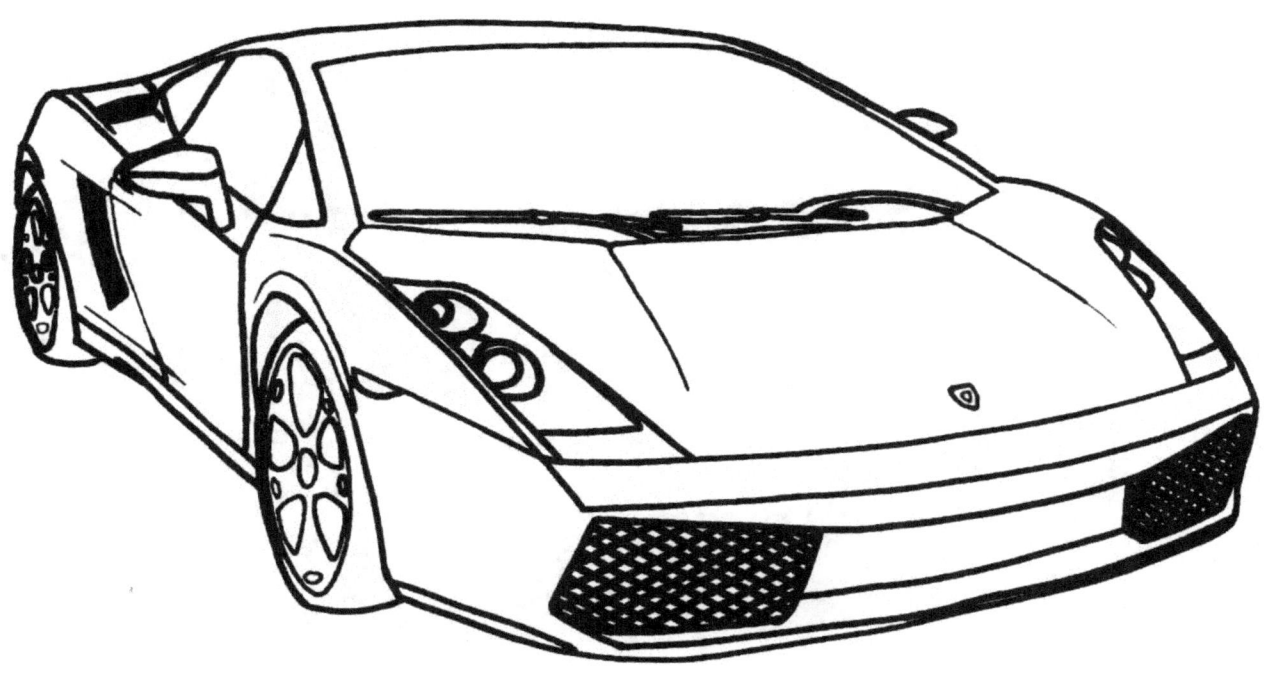

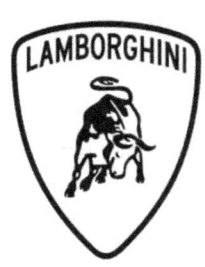

Gallardo
2003 - 2007
Made in Italy